M000204132

Praise for *Driven by Intention*

Driven by Intention is *the* real deal! It's rich with facts and raw truths and overflowing with inspiring stories and insights that show us the power of intention and how we can achieve our dreams through this. Michelle's experience in its own right provides a blueprint to success. *Driven by Intention* has provoked me with new questions and practical steps to reimagine what's next and further sharpen my intention. Thank you for this gift. This gem-filled book is a must-read.

—Esi Eggleston Bracey
COO EVP Unilever Beauty and Personal Care, North America

An empowering and inspirational guide that reveals how professional missteps can become essential lessons rather than fatal setbacks. This book is candid, powerful, and uplifting!

—Robert Livingston
author of *The Conversation* and lecturer
in Public Policy at Harvard Kennedy School

Equal parts inspiring and practical, this is a book to read and reread. Gadsden-Williams has given us a gift.

—Dolly Chugh
Jacob B. Melnick Term Professor at NYU Stern School of Business
and author of *The Person You Mean to Be*

Wisdom is rare and this book has it! Dig in and be inspired and encouraged. Most importantly, there are tools here—tools to bring out the best in you.

—Carmen Rita Wong
former CNBC host and author of *Why Didn't You Tell Me*

In writing *Driven by Intention*, Michelle Gadsden-Williams has developed a wonderful resource for professionals from all walks of life who are committed to bringing their best selves to all aspects of their lives. She presents a powerful take on what it means to contemplate our deepest desires and aspirations and to pursue that "inner voice." Drawing on insights from a variety of renowned leaders and her own decades-long experience as a corporate leader, Gadsden-Williams effectively inspires readers to live life on their own terms even when that contradicts a "socially approved path." She also motivates us to be relentless in pursuing our intentions—no matter how big or small they may appear.

—**Stephanie J. Creary, PhD**
organizational scholar and management professor
at University of Pennsylvania (The Wharton School)

For so many of us, the space between here and now and the future we dream of often feels impossibly wide and discouraging. Michelle Gadsden-Williams gently closes the gap with wise advice and warm encouragement. I am already putting her insights to work!

—**Tricia Rose**
professor at Brown University

Driven by Intention is both thoughtful and instructive. Michelle offers candid personal stories, leadership lessons, and pragmatic, actionable recommendations on how to architect a successful and intentional career. I recommend Michelle's research-based insights to all emerging talent navigating the challenge, opportunity, and privilege of leadership.

—**Kenneth I. Chenault**
chairman and managing director at General Catalyst;
former chairman and CEO of American Express

Driven by Intention is a compilation of candid stories, insights, and practical career advice for the next generation of leaders. The anecdotes shared in this book will help all readers by leveraging intention as the guidepost to become better and more effective leaders. Gadsden-Williams's book is essential reading for anyone interested in disrupting the status quo in their careers.

—Ursula Burns
former CEO and chairwoman of Xerox Corporation and VEON Ltd.

For strategic and practical guidance on navigating their personal lives and careers, young women will find *Driven by Intention* a welcome addition to their toolkits. Michelle Gadsden-Williams shares her inspiring personal story and those of a number of accomplished women who offer insights that will resonate with anyone looking to find purpose and meaning on their own journeys.

—Thasunda Brown Duckett
president and CEO of TIAA

Michelle unravels intention from ambition with a playbook for winning on your own terms. We can all have ambition, yet we win with intention.

—Bonita C. Stewart
VP at Google and coauthor of *A Blessing:*
Women of Color Teaming Up to Lead, Empower and Thrive

Driven by Intention is an actionable, thoughtful, and accessible guide for women who aspire to maximize their professional success and achieve their greatest potential. Michelle Gadsden-Williams and the incredible women interviewed in her book help us realize that the recipe for reaching our fullest potential is teachable, measurable, and achievable. And while the path may not always be easy, it is always worth it. Start with this book.

—Mariana Garavaglia
chief people and business operations officer at Peloton

Driver
by
INTENTION

Driven by INTENTION

OWN YOUR PURPOSE, GAIN POWER, AND PURSUE YOUR PASSION AS A WOMAN AT WORK

MICHELLE GADSDEN-WILLIAMS
with ERIKA ROMAN SAINT-PIERRE

Mc
Graw
Hill

New York   Chicago   San Francisco   Athens   London
Madrid   Mexico City   Milan   New Delhi
Singapore   Sydney   Toronto

Copyright © 2022 by Michelle Gadsden-Williams. All rights reserved. Printed in the United States of America. Except as permitted under the United States Copyright Act of 1976, no part of this publication may be reproduced or distributed in any form or by any means, or stored in a database or retrieval system, without the prior written permission of the publisher.

1 2 3 4 5 6 7 8 9   LCR   27 26 25 24 23 22

ISBN   978-1-260-47391-9
MHID   1-260-47391-0

e-ISBN   978-1-260-47392-6
e-MHID   1-260-47392-9

Library of Congress Cataloging-in-Publication Data

Names: Gadsden-Williams, Michelle – author.
Title: Driven by intention : own your purpose, gain power, and pursue your
    passion as a woman at work / Michelle Gadsden-Williams.
Description: New York : McGraw Hill, [2022] | Includes bibliographical
    references and index.
Identifiers: LCCN 2021051207 (print) | LCCN 2021051208 (ebook) |
    ISBN 9781260473919 (hardback) | ISBN 9781260473926 (ebook)
Subjects: LCSH: Women in the professions. | Women—Psychology. |
    Women—Life skills guides.
Classification: LCC HD6054 .G33 2021 (print) | LCC HD6054 (ebook) |
    DDC 650.1/082—dc23/eng/20211019
LC record available at https://lccn.loc.gov/2021051207
LC ebook record available at https://lccn.loc.gov/2021051208

McGraw Hill books are available at special quantity discounts to use as premiums and sales promotions or for use in corporate training programs. To contact a representative, please visit the Contact Us pages at www.mhprofessional.com.

McGraw Hill is committed to making our products accessible to all learners. To learn more about the available support and accommodations we offer, please contact us at accessibility@mheducation.com. We also participate in the Access Text (www.accesstext.org), and ATN members may submit requests through ATN.

For Mom and Dad

It has been my greatest intention to always make you proud.

Thank you for setting the best example.

Intention is the core
of all conscious life.
Conscious intention colors
and moves everything.

—HSING YUN

CONTENTS

CONTENTS

FOREWORD

Michelle Gadsden-Williams shares moving stories and insights to illustrate how accomplished women employ intention and agility to build meaningful careers and lives.

For many of us, achievement is the expectation of parents, grand-parents, and teachers who set a path for us—the cumulative effect of putting one foot in front of the other, year after year, not so much as a series of choices, but more as the natural result of fulfilling the promise others have seen in us. Just as it is for some of the women in Michelle's book, our imperative is overcoming hardship and finding security; for others of us, it is a desire to attain family approval or to live up to the legacy of generations of high-achieving role models.

Michelle's book is important, not because she has profiled exceptional women (which she has), but because she introduces us to 14 women who model how to weather emotional and intellectual challenges: how to turn adversity into opportunity and how to shape—with intention—our futures.

Though many of the issues Michelle writes about are evergreen, familiar to all who study achievers, the COVID-19 pandemic—and the economic and social upheaval associated with it—has increased the pressure. With the kind of step change we see around us, we will have to reimagine our careers and lives, again and again. To thrive, we must all become discovery-driven learners who can act our way, not plan our way, to the future.

Michelle's book illuminates a truth too many try to deny: Chasing success is a bankrupt activity. The narratives she shares affirm our inner voice that *following our intention is the secret sauce of building a career.* As the journeys she writes about illustrate, intention is about *why* we choose to do what we do and *how* we get it done. This clarity is what leads us to mindful choices and authentic lives.

Michelle's acute ability to listen to these women's stories allows her to distill insights about how we can realize meaningful careers in the face of accelerating change and uncertainty. She introduces us to people who have figured out how to build careers on their own terms despite challenges rising from gender, race, or sexual orientation. Anyone who has grown up in poverty and discrimination knows just how tenuous security and safety can be. The women profiled in this book have learned that the only way to achieve safety and security is to be true to themselves and take calculated risks.

These women have discovered, sometimes the hard way, intention starts with identity—a sense of purpose. Purpose is about something bigger than the self. Early on in the book, Michelle asks each of us to grapple with two existential questions: Who are you? Whom do you serve? She implores us to look in our hearts, not just our heads, to inquire about what really matters to us. What makes you happy? What difference do you want to make in this world? As we read, we are inspired to be ever more ambitious about the problems and opportunities we will tackle with our intentions.

The strategies and tactics embedded in these stories help us figure out how to beat the odds and execute our intentions. As we watch careers unfold in these pages, from first jobs to leadership positions in chosen fields, we see how each journey is about discovering a "unique slice of genius"—a phrase that I learned as I studied leaders at Pixar.

Michelle's book also underscores how our lived experiences shape us. She recounts the experiences of the women as children and asks us to reflect on the lessons of our experiences: What personal gifts did we develop that are now core to our careers? Many in the book recall how, early on, family members and others perceived them as being "different" or having "idiosyncrasies." Michelle describes how instead of denying those differences, the women embrace them—sometimes at great cost—and how that has paid off for the women. They have learned to rely on their unique talents to become "clutch players," as one woman observes about herself, indispensable to their organization's success.

Necessity is a blessing too, Michelle reveals. We watch as the women develop the resilience, tenacity, and work ethic required to deliver exceptional performance and outcomes. They learn early on that the way to overcome people's perceptions of them as "less than" is to become "better than." What makes all the effort and sacrifice worth it? It is not proving others are wrong to underestimate them, but rather it is making progress toward their personal "why," or intention.

Each woman's story is a tale of lifelong learning and self-development. The women profiled in the book are prepared to go beyond their apparent talent and to acquire new mindsets, competencies, and behaviors. In so doing, these women admonish us to strive for excellence, not perfection. Combined with a felt obligation to "represent" their identity group, to never to let them down, perfectionism will make us risk-averse. Bold ambition demands calculated risk taking and mitigation. These women admit their vulnerabilities and identify missteps they have made along the way. They share setbacks, like how it feels to move home to live with parents after holding a big job with all the trappings of success. But the key lesson they share is about how to come back from adversity. It is by reaffirming intention that we can get unstuck and find the energy to move forward.

Fair warning: The career paths of the women introduced here may unnerve you. You will see very little fast tracking. Instead, there are ups and downs, twists and turns. Some of these women take on different roles in different organizations and in different industries. Many of their pivots are the result of deliberate decisions; some, not so much. It is often through serendipity and exposure to a wide range of experiences that they discover their intentions and gain the confidence to lean in and pursue them. Their career paths, some nonlinear, are not surprising. There was one woman whose career was arguably linear— she worked for the same company for her entire career and worked her way to the top! Let's face it: Many women have ended up in positions they did not know even existed when in young adulthood.

As I read about these women, I was struck by how open-minded and opportunistic they are thanks to intention. They seem to trust their choices even in the midst of naysayers. If their only way into a field is to take a step back in their career or accept an entry-level position, they grab it. They use all assignments to showcase their formidable talents and work ethic and deliver results that cause others to take notice. As their intentions become clearer and grow bolder in scope and scale, the women become ever more deliberate in their career and life choices, pursuing the opportunities they need to fulfill their dreams. Their stories encourage us to get out of our comfort zone, to take on stretch assignments that require practicing new versions of our evolving selves.

Through her stories, Michelle shows us how to exercise agency and advocate for ourselves, when others may not recognize our potential. From these women, we learn how to be proactive both in identifying and securing developmental opportunities and in formulating "graceful exit strategies" when our reasonable requests are denied or our value unappreciated.

Driven by Intention is chock-full of examples of discovery-driven learning, fueled by intention. We are encouraged to think of careers as rigorous and relevant experiments from which we can learn and—based on that learning—design and execute the next experiment that will help us grow and solve problems, moving us toward opportunities our intention represents.

Michelle's women grow to love their work and to develop self-confidence and an entrepreneurial mindset—the pursuit of opportunity beyond resources controlled. We watch as they move from being value creators to game changers—individuals whose intentions are not just about what should they be doing, but rather about what could they be doing.

Michelle's stories bring into sharp relief what my research on how leaders learn to lead tells us: *What we know is based on what we get to do; and what we get to do is based on whom we know.* To fulfill intention, we must build relationships. *Varied* experiences collected over the course of a career allow us to develop and practice the contextual intelligence and emotional intelligence required to develop healthy relationships with those very different from themselves. We need experiences that help us learn how to be not only builders, but also translators and bridgers—connecting the diverse individuals and groups we need to develop ourselves and execute on our intentions.

We get a front row seat as the leaders in this book curate and cultivate their own "personal boards of directors," the network of relationships they need to facilitate their learning and effectiveness over the course of their careers. We see how they overcome the challenges underrepresented minorities face in cultivating these relationships and glean insight into how to get others to sponsor, coach, challenge, and protect us. These women are exemplars of individuals who have learned that the challenge is not about finding the "perfect mentor," but rather about being the "perfect protégé" who can attract others to develop them. A senior executive, who had a reputation for sponsoring women, once explained to me what he would look for in the people he chose to mentor—those who were open to feedback and those "who brought him a whale when he sent them out to fish for flounder."

Michelle's stories remind us how important it is to have a diverse set of people in your developmental network. We need allies, individuals who come from demographically different groups from yourself. Michelle includes the story of one of her most important allies, the executive chairman of a Fortune 500 company, a Caucasian man from the Midwest. They met in 2004. When she worked for him, he not only offered private counsel, but also served as a public champion and protector. When faced with tough choices, she still turns to him for feedback and career counseling.

One of the most affirming messages in the book is the extent to which we all must rely on one another—what Michelle refers to as the "sisterhood"—for personal and professional support. Who better to teach us the delicate art of being authentic and still "fitting in"? We see that being authentic is not about disclosing everything we think and feel, but rather about sharing those aspects of who you are and what you stand for to meet your intention—again risky propositions for women and people of color. Michelle shares nuanced advice about how to navigate what can be very difficult conversations.

As the COVID-19 pandemic has reminded us, women face special challenges when it comes to wealth creation and "work-life balance." We are reminded of the importance of developing financial literacy, so we can make sound financial decisions. For sure, wealth offers degrees of freedom that make it easier to live a life of intention. Many of the women in this book have indeed become wealthy by any standard. These are women with demanding careers and formidable energy and a passion for life. The women warn that "work-life balance" can be elusive. They suggest that perhaps you can "have it all," but maybe just not all at the same time. They seem to aspire for an "integrated life," a life that goes beyond work and includes family, friends, and community engagement.

There are no "queen bees" among this group of trailblazers. They are well aware that nothing important gets done alone and that they stand on the shoulders of those who went before them. For Michelle and the majority of the women in this book, their lives are about improving the world, which for sure means doing their part to improve the livelihoods and lives of those like themselves.

I am humbled to be in the company of the women profiled in this book. Many are "hidden figures" in our midst who are making a difference. Like the women featured in her book, Michelle is a woman of intention. This book represents Michelle's 30-year journey to help women and people of color realize their full potential and help corporations deliver on their diversity, equity, and inclusion promises. With this project, Gadsden-Williams is paying forward her father's loving admonishment: "We are not here to occupy space. We are here to make a difference."

Michelle has provided a forum to share hard-earned wisdom. We know from a growing body of research that millennials are committed to building careers of purpose and impact. This book is a playbook based on real-life experience, not theory. It is not too early or too late to reframe careers; we are all living and working longer. We all aspire to have more integrated and fulfilling lives—and work takes up so much of our precious time. Savor the stories in this book. They help us make the space to reflect on where we have been and what that tells us about where we want to go and how we can get there. Think of the women in this book as life coaches walking alongside us as we cocreate our individual and collective futures.

Linda A. Hill
Wallace Brett Donham Professor of Business Administration at the Harvard Business School and Chair of the Leadership Initiative. Dr. Hill is coauthor of the award-winning books *Being the Boss: The 3 Imperatives for Becoming a Great Leader* (with Kent Lineback) and *Collective Genius: The Art and Practice of Leading Innovation* (with Greg Brandeau, Emily Truelove, and Kent Lineback).

ACKNOWLEDGMENTS

Writing a book felt different the second time around. This time, the focus was on 14 incredibly successful individuals whom I did not want to disappoint. There were fits and starts, as I was acutely aware that someone might just pick up this book and read what I had to say, which left me second-guessing each chapter. Thankfully, I decided to let the process work and the words flow, and I am extremely proud of the end result . . . and I hope that all 14 are equally as proud of their contribution to this book.

First, I'd like to thank David and my family for giving me the time and space to dedicate to this project. Thank you for your unconditional love, patience, and unwavering support throughout this process . . . not to mention reading every page and providing input. Everything I do . . . I do it for you!

My literary agent, Regina Brooks, played an integral part in helping me to crystalize the idea and concept for this second book and providing me with sound counsel every step of the way. You always had the right words and provided me with a sense of confidence as we entered new territory and found a new publishing home. There aren't enough words to express my gratitude.

To my publishers, McGraw Hill/Open Lens, and to Marva Allen, Marie Brown, Regina Brooks, and Cheryl Segura. Thank you for your belief in this project from its inception. I am fortunate to have such a gifted team surrounding me from start to finish. Your strategic direction, feedback, and coaching along the way have been immeasurable.

To Erika Roman Saint-Pierre, my collaborator, it has been pure joy and a gift to have you as my partner on this journey. Your enthusiasm for this project from the beginning was infectious. It has been a real pleasure working with you on this book. Thank you for lending your expertise in helping me to stay the course, be well organized, and above all else represent the protagonists of this book with impeccable grace and elegance.

To Philana Patterson, you are a gem! Your keen eye and sharpness in terms of sentence structure, flow, and language have made me a better writer. Your advice and expertise have been invaluable. Thank you for taking the time to help me with this project.

I am fortunate to work for BlackRock, an amazing company with an extraordinary group of executives and employees who are nothing short of supportive of my external endeavors—namely this book. Special thanks to Larry Fink, Chairman and Chief Executive Officer; Rob Kapito, President; and Manish Mehta, Chief Human Resources Officer, and to the Global Executive Committee, the Human Resource Leadership Team, and the entire BlackRock community for their support of this book. It is my greatest honor to serve as your Global Head of Diversity, Equity and Inclusion.

Last but certainly not least, I want to thank the individuals I interviewed for this book—who shared their unvarnished, truthful stories and anecdotes: Marie Forleo, Alex Gorsky, Arlan Hamilton, Mellody Hobson, Georgene Huang, Minyon Moore, Romy Newman, Michele

Roberts, Sheri Salata, Dia Simms, Davia Temin, Mimi Valdés, Alexa von Tobel, Angela Yee, and Linda Hill who wrote the Foreword. This book would not have been possible without your contribution. The courage, vulnerable stories, and wisdom that you each shared will be appreciated by the readers. You've given them a gift!

INTRODUCTION

Know thyself.

—PLATO

I've worked for some of the world's biggest and most influential corporations, Accenture, Credit Suisse, Merck, and Novartis among them. As I write this, I am serving as managing director and global head of diversity, equity, and inclusion at investment management firm BlackRock, which oversees more than $9 trillion in assets for retail and institutional investors.

Early in my career, when I was working as a staffing and diversity analyst at Wakefern Food Corporation, I was selected to help the CEO and the chief operating officer create a presentation for the co-op members. At the time, PowerPoint, which has become a common tool for doing presentations, was fairly new to this company, and it was also very new to me. I was home working on the presentation for the senior leadership and I could see that something wasn't going right. I stopped what I was doing and went to the office at 10 p.m. to work on it. I stayed there overnight and worked with the IT team to fix the problem. Finally, by 5 a.m. the presentation was ready, and I was able to go back home, get ready for work, and make a U-turn back to the office.

I didn't initially tell my boss about the technical problem or coming in and staying all night to fix it. I just showed up and said, "Here's the presentation." The chief operating officer presented it without a hitch—it was flawless. Afterward, I got a thank you and firm handshake from the CEO and several of his direct reports. It was a proud moment for me; I was a star. My intention was not only to do a great job, but to prove to the people in leadership that I was trustworthy and someone that they could count on to get the job done well—by any means necessary. Weeks later, I did tell my boss about what it took to get the presentation done. I focused on the result versus the odds that I faced.

Have you ever stopped to consider what intention is and the role it plays in your life? Intention is a choice with commitment. It starts with understanding your "why." It's a spark that ignites the fire within each of us not only to have an aim or a goal and deliver on it, but to be planful and purposeful about it. It's a clear representation of our deepest desires and who we aspire to be. More importantly, it addresses why you want to do something and how you will do it. Simply said, it is our motivation. It's that inner voice that guides our every whim. It is an unshakable desire to be a goal setter, a dream chaser, and an impact seeker with equal emphasis on "why" and "how." Intention distinguishes those who truly seek their goals from those who get stuck when they encounter obstacles, unable to strategically move past them.

Why is intention so important? Intention requires us to hold ourselves to a higher standard and is accountable for making things happen in our lives. It means deconstructing our successes and failures and taking and using those life lessons to guide us to our North Star, the ultimate intention that drives us. Intention requires us to do the things that often scare us. Greatness demands purpose. Failure is not trying.

Everything that I do—and have done—is by *my* design. There hasn't been one major decision that I've made that was not purposeful or planned, whether it was to get married in my twenties, to aspire to become vice president of a major multinational corporation in my thirties, to work and live as an expat in Switzerland, to write a book (now two!), or to start my own business—Ceiling Breakers LLC.

Nothing in my career has happened by mistake. Yes, there have been missteps, including not listening to wise counsel, not always speaking up and asking for what I wanted, and not thinking carefully through the consequences of my actions as a leader. I embrace my missteps, miscalculations, or any shortcomings as life lessons; every risk has been a reward worth taking.

Intentionality was something instilled in my two sisters and me by our parents—especially my father. Growing up, my father always said, "We are not here to occupy space. We are here to make a difference. It's up to each of us to determine what that difference is." His words "We are here to make a difference" have stayed with me over the years as a credo I live by. I strongly believe that our thoughts and our intentions create our reality.

Every morning before school, my father asked my sisters and me the same three questions, "So, girls, what do you want to do? What do you want to be? Where do you want to go?"

We were in primary school when this started, and looking back, those were pretty sophisticated questions to ask us. Asking those questions over and over again was my father's way of nurturing our talents and teaching us the importance of articulating our desires in an intentional way. Those questions served as a foundation for the skills I developed: the intentionality in how I think about my life, my career, and who I am.

In the spirit of the questions my father asked me daily, I make it a point at the beginning of each year to take time to answer the following questions for myself:

- What do I want?
- What are my gifts?
- What gives me fulfillment?
- What attributes or qualities do I enjoy expressing to the world?
- What is my intuition telling me to do?
- Is it worth the risk?

Take a few minutes and write down the answers to these questions for yourself. Even if you've done this exercise before, repeating it helps to reinforce your motivation and solidify your intention. Having your "how" and "why "in the forefront of your mind keeps you from deviating from your path.

How and *what* you do informs *why* you do it. I am driven by my convictions, and I am extremely clear about the why of my intention.

For most of my career, I was able to accomplish my goals in a relatively short period of time. I'm sure you're probably asking, "How did you do this?" And here is my response, encapsulated in four bullet points:

- I made my career aspirations known to all who could make them happen—my manager, human resources, senior executives, mentors, and sponsors. I stated them aloud to myself and to those who held the power in their hands. I knew I wanted to work abroad at some point in my career, so I always chose to work for multinational organizations. But I knew I had to do more than just be in the right places.

Any opportunity I had to talk to those who had influence in making that happen—I would let them know.

- I created a vision board that illustrated not just what I wanted to do, but also when and why I wanted to do it, along with the necessary steps to take to achieve it. A lot of vision boards focus on images that represent our intentions. My vision board included timelines and clear steps with dates for when I wanted to achieve my goals.

- I leveraged my ecosystem of power players who would give me sage advice. I was aggressive about forming relationships with mentors and sponsors. I would walk into someone's office who had a skill that I admired and ask, "Would you be my mentor?" It worked out very well. My mentors are Ann M. Fudge, former chairman and CEO of Young & Rubicam Brands; Alex Gorsky, the executive chairman of Johnson & Johnson; Thomas Ebeling, former CEO of Novartis Pharma; and Paulo Costa, who was the CEO of Janssen and Novartis Pharma before Alex, just to name a few. No one has ever said no to me. Perhaps people were shocked that I would walk up and ask. I figured the worst that could happen was they could say no.

- I didn't just "push through" when life dealt me setbacks out of my control. Around 2005, I began having bouts of fatigue, low-grade fevers, headaches, and stiffness and swelling around my joints. I found it difficult to get out of bed. Every morning when I combed my hair, there would be clumps of hair left behind in the teeth of the comb. After I was finally diagnosed with lupus and years later rheumatoid arthritis, two chronic autoimmune diseases, I worked with my doctors and engaged experts—my medical team and a life coach—to help me get back to better health and develop habits and strategies that would allow me to continue working toward my goals despite my health challenges.

Intention extends far beyond having an ambition—or the courage to ask the top person at your company to mentor you. It requires you to be extremely conscious about the career choices and decisions you make in executing your life plan. In some circles, intention has come to be accepted as the law of attraction—attracting the people we want in our lives and the things that we want to acquire that we are convinced will bring us contentment. It's this notion that if we really desire something, the universe conspires to give it to us. I propose that there should also be sincere, deliberate effort in our actions. Leading our lives with intention requires having a year-round, lifelong action plan. Our motives and actions manifest our intentions. My daily mantra is, "Intention without deliberate words and calculated action is meaningless."

As a chief diversity officer for more than 25 years across several multinational companies, I've had the opportunity to work with a range of professionals from recent college grads to CEOs. I'm passionate about working with millennials given their commitment to tackle issues that matter to them; the professional choices they make are rooted in their core values, shaping how the world operates.

One of my intentions is to help the next generation of women leaders realize their ambition and potential. Over the years, I've spent countless hours with young professionals providing advice on how to navigate their careers. One of the many things that I admire about millennial women (ages 27 to 41 in 2021) is how courageous and confident they are, more so than baby boomers (between 57 and 77 years old) and Gen Xers (between 42 and 56 years old).[1] Millennial women are more highly educated than previous generations and are entering the workforce in higher numbers, according to research from professional services firm PwC.[2] Each day, I am surrounded by these wonderfully gifted and talented professionals who know exactly what they want. However, they are looking for strategic guidance on how to reach their North Star—their guiding aspiration—whatever that may be. Put another way, your North Star is your goal, and intention is how you get there.

HOW TO USE THIS BOOK

Driven by Intention is a playbook that connects attaining your goals with finding purpose and meaning in your career. Through the stories of and advice from women that I sat down with for interviews, you'll learn what it means to set an intention that helps you find fulfillment in your career and personal life. If you've ever felt marginalized or been told that your dreams are "too big," this is your motivational guide. I wrote this book for people like you who have the audacity to remain true to your core and realize your ambition despite the naysayers.

Within these pages you will find steps that you can tailor to fit your circumstances. Each chapter includes exercises to assist you in building your personal action plan. I encourage you to stop and write down the questions I ask and as well write down your answers. Writing things down is a powerful action. If you take the time to commit your answers to paper, you are more likely to act on your findings. You may even want to grab a notebook or journal before you move on to the first chapter so you'll be ready!

If you read my book *Climb: Taking Every Step with Conviction, Courage, and Calculated Risk to Achieve a Thriving Career and Successful Life*, you've likely explored some of these concepts through my story. As I marveled at the response to *Climb* and reflected on the successes of women that I know and the challenges others are facing, I wanted to broaden the lens. My story is relevant for many women, but what about those who didn't have similar socioeconomic backgrounds, influences, interests, or career fields? You'll find a range of women in this book whose backgrounds show that with intention, you can have the life and career that you desire. If you believe that something about you or your circumstances precludes you from the life you want, think again.

I set out to talk to a diverse group of women about their intentions and the thought processes, actions, and courage that have helped them chart their paths. Some of these women are my old friends, and others are new. You'll learn about the inspiring successes (and occasional stumbles) of real working women, some of the most successful women of our day.

In these pages you'll meet powerful women including, but not limited to:

- Mellody Hobson, president and co-CEO of the largest Black-owned asset management firm, Ariel Investments. You may think you don't know Mellody, but you probably do. She's one of the preeminent experts called on by media to help explain money matters to the masses.
- Cofounders of Fairygodboss Georgene Huang, CEO, and Romy Newman, president. The former coworkers are among the growing ranks of female founders shaking up corporate America—and they're doing it by helping other women succeed.
- Dia Simms, who worked under one of the world's leading recording executives and entrepreneurs. The former president of Combs Enterprises, Dia helped the enterprise grow a number of businesses and played a key role in a deal that vaulted Cîroc vodka's profile in the spirits industry.
- Sheri Salata, who had extraordinary success over more than 20 years with media and entertainment powerhouse Oprah Winfrey. During her time with Oprah, Sheri served as executive producer of *The Oprah Winfrey Show* and president of Winfrey's Harpo Studios.
- Angela Yee, who went from hosting two shows on satellite radio to becoming cohost of the wildly popular, nationally

syndicated morning show *The Breakfast Club,* which has become a must-visit show for entertainers, businesspeople, and political figures seeking to reach diverse millennials.

The personal stories of these and the other passionate, powerful, and purposeful women in this book also highlight the fact that finding meaning in life and fulfillment in your career takes more than just intellectual horsepower and drive. It's about actively working toward something that will ultimately create impact—making a difference in the lives of others.

As you proceed through these pages, you'll find that chapters closer to the end provide nuts-and-bolts advice about getting coaching and managing your finances—two things that I believe are key to manifesting your intention. This book wouldn't be complete without insights from my mentor Alex Gorsky, executive chairman at Johnson & Johnson. His career and leadership at one of the world's largest pharmaceutical and consumer products makers, has given him the opportunity to work with and mentor many women. Think of Alex's chapter as a one-on-one mentoring session, and receive much of what I have from years of advice and counsel from him.

Each chapter of this book ends with practical tips and advice from the people interviewed that you can use in your own life and career. Some of it underscores themes previously touched on in the chapter, and in some cases you'll find new concepts and advice to add to your arsenal.

Finally, we'll reflect on the "red thread" that runs through the experiences and insights of the people featured in this book. For many of you working in business, this term may be familiar. If not, let me explain that a red thread is a constant underlying theme. Understanding what the red threads are helps leaders understand connections and commonalities to answer tough questions.

My hope is that the lessons shared candidly in each chapter will help the next generation of women leaders develop the moxie to live on their own terms and realize that their personal and professional success begins and ends with them—no one else. Sometimes you need to conjure up the courage to circumvent your circumstances and to invest wholeheartedly in yourself. You just have to trust your instincts and be strategic about your next steps. This book is designed to help you do that!

1

YOUR MOVE

Setting Intentions Versus Setting Goals

Our intention creates our reality.
—WAYNE DYER

At this point, you may be asking yourself, "Why should I identify and set an intention?"

Intention is critical in creating the life that nourishes you personally and professionally. It helps you strategically make moves and shifts to get into the right position, not only for your career but for the spaces where you live and play. As we talk to a range of groundbreakers, pacesetters, and innovators, we'll also explore different elements of living your intention, something far different from compiling and checking off to-do lists.

When we talk about setting goals and setting intentions, some people may think they are the same. The truth is that they are two very distinct concepts that work hand in hand to guide you in creating your ideal life. That's not to say goals aren't an important part of intention, because the two work in tandem. But goals aren't the end-all, be-all of creating the life you desire.

SETTING AN INTENTION VERSUS SETTING GOALS

What's the difference between goals and intentions? It's been said that goals are focused on the future, while intentions are in the present moment. Expressed another way, goals are fixed or specific, whereas intentions are fluid and ongoing from day to day.

In short, intention is *why* you want to do something, and goals are *how* you will do it. Intention breeds goals, and goals help push your intention to fruition. To illustrate my point, here's an example about chess. Let's say you want to become a chess champion. That is your intention. Winning a game of chess is a goal that brings you closer to your overall intention of being a champion.

But why focus on intention over goals? Goals are concrete. The human mind has been socially conditioned, for hundreds of years, to think in terms of goal setting. Think about the last time you hit a milestone—a goal that was pretty big, such as getting your first senior or executive position. It felt huge, right? But then after the initial "I did it!" wore off, what was left? The goal was achieved, and you were proud. But it's a short-lived joy, and it can leave you feeling empty, asking, "What's next for me?"

Let's also discuss what happens when you don't achieve a goal. You can feel like a failure. You lose motivation. You may feel like giving up altogether. There's a point where you achieve a goal, or you don't—there's no wiggle room.

In her *Inc.* magazine article, "Setting Goals Isn't Enough: Setting Daily Intentions Will Change Your Life," business coach Marla Tabaka sings the praises of an intention-setting life. "Setting and living your intentions allows you to focus on who you are in the moment, to recognize and live your values, and to raise your emotional energy, which in turn raises your physical energy," she writes. "Many entrepreneurs are excellent at identifying their values and know that living within their interpretation of them is a powerful way to achieve success, and more importantly, happiness."[1]

> Intention breeds goals, and goals help push your intention to fruition.

4

Intentions keep us in the present moment where our lives are being lived, not in the future where goals can seem out of reach and nebulous.

As we meet businesspeople throughout this book, you'll start to see how an intention-led life manifests a successful career and a life that you can live to the fullest every day.

In the Introduction of this book and in my previous work, *Climb*, I shared my story around intention. For me, the concept of setting an intention was ingrained in my life early. That's not the case for everyone, but it doesn't mean you can't set intentions later in life and achieve success. You can even create a career around helping millions of people live a more intentional life—like Sheri Salata. If you've ever felt like you've misstepped or that it's too late to start again, you'll want to pay close attention to Sheri's story.

MEET SHERI SALATA

Author, speaker, and producer Sheri Salata is an expert when it comes to transforming lives, and that includes her own. However, Sheri didn't know that she would find a dream job working with one of the most recognized and successful women on the planet, Oprah Winfrey.

Sheri says early achievement played a role in how she began to understand success.

"There was a lot of validation that came with achievement, and I got looped into that very early on," she recalls. "I don't know exactly, maybe it was fourth grade, my teacher gave me extra books because I was a good reader: the *Little House on the Prairie* series. I started to see that accomplishing and achieving came with lots of rewards, rewards that I wanted."

As the oldest grandchild in her family, Sheri often found herself babysitting her young cousins. She would create television shows and "boss everybody around." She didn't know it then, but those "shows" would foreshadow an unimaginable career and life success.

It would take a while for that success to manifest. Like many of us, Sheri had developed a specific vision of what success looked like. That vision was very different from the life and career she ultimately achieved.

"I knew I wanted to do well. I knew I wanted to be 'successful.' I think my definition of being successful was immature at the time. It was having a snappy business card and a cool title and the fancy brief-case and all the meetings . . . I wanted the trappings of what it would feel like to be successful in the world."

With that, Sheri set out on a quest to find that "successful" career. While in college, she almost failed out of pre-med, so she switched to marketing because it seemed doable and wouldn't interrupt what she calls her "party train." She didn't have any interest in her finance and sta-tistics classes, but a degree in marketing would bring that "briefcase–business card" vision of success to life, so that's what she pursued.

After graduating from college, Sheri took a host of jobs, not cer-tain of what she wanted to do, but ever moving toward that briefcase–business card vision of success, until she found herself as manager for the convenience store chain 7-Eleven.

Sheri hadn't fallen on tough times—at least not yet. At the time, 7-Eleven was headquartered in an impressive, mirrored building in Dallas, Texas.

"Everybody wanted to get to the gleaming towers, but you had to start in the stores. So I literally went through the 7-Eleven manager training program for eight months, the hardest eight months of my life," she says.

What was so hard about it?

"They trained you in a smaller store, meaning there was only one person in the store at the time," she recalls. She did a little bit of every-thing: from creating a cash report, running the register, making coffee, changing drink tanks, stocking shelves—even cleaning the Slurpee machine.

"And then maybe you'd get to leave by four in the morning," she says.

Sheri stuck with it, and her persistence paid off. She was promoted to supervisor. She was able to ditch the uniform and drive around "in my little car with my little briefcase and see all the managers."

She was closer to the goal of working in the gleaming towers. She figured she would continue rising and then retire someday. Everything was on track.

Sheri was about to get promoted to a bigger job, but she was burning out.

"I just burst into tears," she says. "And I was like, I've got to quit. And they're like, 'What?'"

This wasn't the only time Sheri's plan to achieve her vision of success crashed and burned. She would find herself in a "good" job with "good" insurance and a 401(k) plan, but in her soul she was desperately unhappy. "I would make the best of a bad situation until I couldn't get out of bed in the morning. And those months turned into years. I'd get so miserable, I'd have to quit. And again. And then again. It was that way in my twenties and early thirties, because I didn't like what I was doing."

EXPLORING OPTIONS AND REIMAGINING YOUR LIFE

Now you may think we're at the point in Sheri's story when she joined *The Oprah Winfrey Show* and became its executive producer and co-president of Harpo Studios and OWN, the Oprah Winfrey Network. Not yet. Before any of that happened, Sheri landed somewhere that most people never want to go back to as an adult—her parents' basement.

Few people feel great about returning home to live with their parents after they've gone away to college or started careers, but it's becoming more and more common. Millions of young people are temporarily taking residence in their childhood bedroom as they go to college, save money, pay off student debt, and climb the corporate ladder. The COVID-19 pandemic exacerbated this trend. Fifty-two percent, or 26.6 million, of people aged 18–29 lived with one or both of their parents in July 2020, according to an analysis of census data done by the Pew Research Center. In February 2020, before the pandemic, 47 percent, or 24 million, of people in the 18–29 cohort already lived with one or both parents. The average length of stay for college-educated millennials who have returned home is three years, and it is significantly higher for their less-educated counterparts.[2]

"I lived in the basement with my dog, Addie Lou, and just kind of felt like a real failure. I was 27. Everybody else is much further along in their careers and their lives. And now I'm back and living with my parents with no money," Sheri says.

Even if it provides a little breathing room to choose what comes next, going back home can shake your confidence. In fact, for 75 percent of young adults, success is defined as financial autonomy.[3] Sheri certainly experienced those feelings as she started this new chapter of her life, "I could feel that I wasn't where people thought I should be. I wasn't happy myself with where I was," she remembers.

Returning home gave her the space she needed to remember that long forgotten childhood attraction to producing television. For Sheri, this is where the intention that would shape some of the most transformative years of her life kicked in. Sheri managed to quiet the critics—including herself.

She had a friend who was engaged to an executive producer at an advertising agency. He offered to take her to lunch "to be nice." He was about 20 years older and had a storied career in advertising. She recalls thinking it sounded like it was a cool job—producing, shooting, editing, choosing music, and creating the television spots. She was broke and needed the income. He asked her what she wanted to do. She replied, "I want to do what you do."

He offered her a job as an entry-level secretary, a step back in her career. It also didn't pay well—just $16,000 a year. "I just was willing to bet on myself that if I took this job making $16,000 a year, I had access to learn how to produce and that I could make it into gold," she says. Eventually, her boss started taking her to shoots for commercials and music sessions. She loved the problem-solving aspect of the job. "It feels like art and some science," she says.

Sheri felt challenged and happy working on an array of commercials for a wide variety of clients including banks and amusement parks for six years. Still, she felt something stirring inside of her; that was what led her to Oprah.

LISTENING TO YOURSELF AND LEADING WITH INTENTION

In her memoir, *The Beautiful No: And Other Tales of Trial, Transcendence, and Transformation*, Sheri recounts how she landed the job on daytime's biggest show.[4] She applied at *The Oprah Winfrey Show* for a job as promo producer. Promo producers put together the 30-second ads that entice viewers to tune in. With her experience in advertising, it seemed like a great fit. She sent her résumé and a video-cassette of her top TV commercials to the head of the department. For weeks, she waited for a call. She finally received a message on her answering machine, "Sorry, you're not what we are looking for."

It was a terrible blow—and there were tears. But Sheri says she wasn't totally shocked. "I had applied on a lark. Now I turned my attention back to advertising and began to freelance as a producer," she says. "I wasn't too good at it though. Soon I was broke again, but then I got an interview at a prestigious agency."

All went well with the interview, and she was told that she would hear back from the folks at the agency in a few days. A few days turned into two weeks, and then the rejection letter arrived. Another blow.

A short time later, when she was 35 years old and had been out of college for 14 years, Sheri got call from someone at *Oprah* who wanted to know if she was interested in doing some freelance work.

> "Be willing to start over as many times as it takes to create the life of your dreams."

Sheri refers to the series of events that led her to *Oprah* as the "beautiful no"—which guided the vision of her memoir. In the book, Sheri implores us to take the time to recognize the beauty in a no and to unearth the gift in rejection. If Sheri had landed that senior producer position, she wouldn't have been available to freelance at the show.

She remembers the day she started as a promo producer at *Oprah* in 1995 in the show's tenth season as the greatest day of her life "because I knew inside those walls of Harpo Studios that I had moved out of just having a job, that my calling had been ignited. I was exactly where I was supposed to be."

And here's the big lesson about intention: It comes and evolves with time. Sure, many people may think 35 is late in the game to be figuring out what you want to do. But you can rest assured, it's never too late when it comes to intention, because it develops and grows with you. It's an entirely bespoke experience, unique to you. Having all those experiences before getting that first job with Oprah made Sheri appreciate it all the more. She knew she was where she needed to be at the exact right moment in her life. Sheri's life is a testament to not giving up, or to, in her words, "be willing to start over as many times as it takes to create the life of your dreams."

Armed with her trademark drive and gusto, after joining the show Sheri strove to do the job she was hired to do better than anyone else. She led with intention, rather than looking at getting the job as a goal achieved. Instead of making promotion her next goal, Sheri took some great advice from a former boss, who told her: "Just do the job in front of you. Don't worry about promotions. Don't worry about being elevated. Just do what you were hired to do." Putting all your focus on doing the job well will naturally bring the rest, the accolades, the promotions, and the advancement with it.

Sheri translated that entry-level promo producer job into becoming the final executive producer of *The Oprah Winfrey Show* and, soon after, the president of Harpo Studios. After *The Oprah Winfrey Show* ended its 25-year run, Sheri continued on as co-president of OWN until 2016. She's stayed busy since then, writing her bestselling memoir and speaking at conferences and innovation summits.

INTENTION: DREAM PRACTICE VERSUS GOAL PRACTICE

Sheri has a beautiful way of looking at intention; she says: "For me, intention is dreaming the outcome before it happens. And a result of setting intention is that you literally create a vibrational climate that surrounds your endeavor." In essence, she sees an outcome, and in doing so, it creates an environment for the right intention to come into being. Part of creating that environment is finding the language that fits you and what you want to manifest.

Sheri recognizes that she wasn't initially driven by goal setting because "I didn't like the language of that, because it feels very masculine to me. And in many ways, because of my generation—when I was in leadership roles, I could be like, 'Oh my God, I'm such a man right now, pushing the rock up the hill and doing the goal setting.'" Instead, Sheri has a more malleable approach to bringing her intention to life. "There are ways that we organize and structure our lives and our dreams. I think putting some goals down for different areas of your life can be useful. It can help you stir up some consciousness around different areas of your life. If you're kind of digging in and wondering, 'What do I really want here?,' I prefer to do a dream practice rather than a goal practice, just because I liked the language better and the words matter to my creative process." Sheri follows her intention by way of her dream practice, where she takes 15 minutes per day to check in with herself and see how she feels about her dreams. She asks herself where she's going, and what does she want it to be or look like. In this way she is taking time every day to revisit her intention, keeping it top of mind with energy bringing it to life in the present.

HOW INTENTION INFORMS A LIFE—BEING YOUR OWN CURATOR AND BOUNCER

One of the many nuggets of wisdom I took away from my time with Sheri was the importance of being your own curator, deciding what you want in your life. She talked at length about this, holding the idea that we are all both curator and doorman, creating and protecting this vision we have for our lives. "I'm the doorman. I'm the bouncer. I decide who gets in and who doesn't. I decide what content gets in, what music I want to hear, what shows I want to watch, what books I want to read. To be sloppy about all that is a drastic error, because you are literally creating your life." Personal responsibility is the crux of creating intention and manifesting the life you wish to live.

CHOOSING YOUR OWN LANGUAGE, MAKING YOUR OWN RULES, CREATING YOUR OWN VISION

You know about intention and goals and how they differ. Sheri's story tells us that we can find our intention at any time and that it is always evolving. Now let's talk about how you can start actively working on yours.

One thing I really love about Sheri's entire philosophy toward life and intention is the way she recognizes that you have to use the language that is native to you and adopt the principles you believe in. For example, as a very successful powerhouse, Sheri has sat on a lot of panels, and she would always get the dreaded question about maintaining work-life balance. Instead of stumbling around the expectations of others, Sheri dismisses it for something she resonates with more organically, saying: "I don't believe in it. I always used to get that question when I'd do panels, how do you maintain a work-life balance? And I was working 80 hours a week, and I felt a lot of shame about that. It was embarrassing. And then I finally thought, 'What do I believe in?' Do I believe in that concept, in that language, in that construct? And the answer is I don't . . . So I took that concept and that language, and I recognized that it's not in any way close to me in my life. And I don't search for it. I'm not looking for that. What I am looking for is that integrated life. This is a life where you have a strong foundation of self-care, where you know yourself, you honor yourself, you have reverence for how you spend your time. Then you're going to make the right decisions for yourself about all those things. You're going to flow your attention to the things in life that make you happy." That is living with intention.

Above all, for Sheri, personal happiness is the guide. You decide what makes you happy. You decide the rules you need to live by to be happy. It's not a one-size-fits-all situation. As she says, "Everybody's gotta find their own recipe. You know, it's a pinch of this, a pinch of that."

SHERI'S ADVICE TO LIVE YOUR LIFE WITH INTENTION

#1: Do the Job in Front of You and Do It Well

There's a lot to be said for staying in the present. Sheri reflects on the greatest advice she ever received from the former boss who advised her to do the job in front of her and not worry about promotions. "I think a lot of times young people are so anxious and eager to be somebody, that they miss the fact that they're supposed to be doing this, learning this, and having this experience," she says. The best way to climb the ladder quickly is to build a reputation as the woman who gets the job done and does it better than anyone else. While it's natural to want to get promoted as quickly as possible, you can only do that by mastering your current position. You'll be building on a strong foundation instead of a shaky one.

#2: Find Your Thing and Follow That Direction

As you'll see as you read this book, some of my featured experts knew at an early age what they wanted from life. Not only did they know what they wanted to do, but they'd also already figured out how to make it happen. However, for some people, like Sheri, it's not as easy. She had eight different jobs after college before landing a junior position at *The Oprah Winfrey Show* at age 35. If it takes longer to determine your intention, that's normal.

#3: Let Happiness Be Your Compass

What is it that Americans are supposed to be doing? According to the Declaration of Independence we should be pursuing our happiness! Let happiness be your true North Star instead of fear or obligation. At 56 years old, Sheri realized that she needed to make happiness her compass, her North Star. "As you chart your career path, surround yourself with those who uplift you, pay attention to the energy that you bring into a room, and pay attention to the energy that comes into a room with other people." If you find that energy doesn't make you happy, change it or leave the room, but whatever you do, stay committed to happiness.

#4: Be Willing to Start Over

Life throws us curveballs, and sometimes things won't work out. Instead of focusing on a perceived failure, reframe it and be grateful for the lesson. Then start over and do it as many times as you need to. Sheri talks about her personal experience, saying, "No matter how successful I was in my other jobs before I found the career I was meant for, I was willing to start over as many times as it took until I found 'the thing.'"

By the way, "the thing" often evolves with you, so you need to be fluid and flexible with yourself. You may end up starting over repeatedly, because with each experience you have, you evolve, and so does your intention.

#5: Dream Your Desired Outcome into Existence

Ever wished you could just think something into being? Well according to Sheri, you can. She says: "Setting an intention is like dreaming the outcome before it happens. I see now that being a curator, being that personal leader of yourself in your health, your relationships, and your professional life, is your real work." You have control over how your day goes, and you have control over how your life goes. You just need to set the intention and let all things flow to and from it.

#6: Exercise Radical Self-Care

Radical self-care is the belief that you need to take care of yourself before you take care of others. It all comes back to self-initiated maintenance of health and well-being, like "Put your mask on first" and "You must fill your cup first and then give the overflow to others." In short, make yourself a priority. Sheri says, "This is a new liberating understanding of being self-ish and self-concerned." That doesn't mean being self-centered or self-involved, but it does mean that you understand that you can only perform at your best when you've taken proper care of yourself. Sheri promises, "Radical self-care is the foundation of everything. If you get it now, your life will be dramatically different."

2

DIFFICULT DECISIONS

Facing the Swerve

Your life changes the moment you make a new,
congruent, and committed decision.
—TONY ROBBINS

Some of you know what I mean when I talk about "facing the swerve," but there may be many of you who are scratching your heads asking, "What's she talking about?"

The art of the swerve is adopting a fluid approach, but still being very focused and intentional, to achieve your goals. Instead of believing that there is one road to get where you want to be, the swerve invites you to embrace the fact that taking a different path from the one you planned may be the better path to fulfill your goals and dreams.

No, intentionality doesn't mean going in a straight line. Sometimes, there are twists and turns and even the unexpected as you move toward your North Star.

HOW DID THE SWERVE ORIGINATE?

The idea of the swerve first entered into the mainstream by a tweet from New York writer Rachel Syme. Ruminating on where she was in her life on the morning of her thirty-sixth birthday, Syme, whose writing has appeared in numerous publications including *New York*, *Elle*, and *GQ*, tweeted: "I feel like 33–38 is a really tough age for a lot of women I know; feels like so many big decisions and future plans have been squeezed into this lil window; . . . It just feels like all my friends this year are doing a huge reevaluation of everything. It's a time of lurches and swerves."

What a big statement for a short tweet! It acknowledges there is this looming deadline to get things done and to do them in a particular way, especially for women in their thirties. Embracing the swerve is reevaluating where you are, where you are going, and what most heightens your passion. Once you determine that, you swerve in the direction that works for where you are in your life now, rather than what you initially envisioned. This idea resonated with both women and men because there is so much societal pressure to "check off the boxes" such as dream jobs, marriage, children, homeownership, ad infinitum. The discussion that followed acknowledged that plans and desires change. What you plan for in your twenties may not be where you want to go in your thirties and beyond. The swerve became a popular term, so popular, in fact, that it was used by the former first lady of the United States, Michelle Obama.

Michelle Obama is the epitome of drive, laser focus, and hard work. It's no surprise that as a young girl, Obama had already constructed a plan for her life that she followed to the letter. However, when interviewed by Stephen Colbert for O magazine, she told him the one person who had changed her life was her husband, President Barack Obama, but the reason why may be surprising.

"Before I met Barack, I was all about checking off the next box—law school, law firm, and nice car," she told Colbert. "But he taught me the art of the swerve, how to take life as it comes, and follow your passions wherever they lead."

Obama left her career as a lawyer and moved onto a career in nonprofits, also working at the University of Chicago and the University of Chicago Medical Center along the way. After her husband's historic White House win, she became an advocate for veterans, military families, education for girls, healthy eating, and addressing the obesity epidemic as first lady—and she's done it with a spirit of excellence.

Clearly, she's mastered the art of the swerve. Another woman who I believe has mastered the art of the swerve while maintaining an intention of excellence is Dia Simms.

MEET DIA SIMMS

I met Dia Simms at the 2016 EssenceFest in New Orleans. If you aren't familiar with EssenceFest, it is a festival put on by *Essence* magazine, and going to it has grown into an annual (not including the period impacted by the COVID-19 virus) pilgrimage; the event includes concerts, parties, motivational and educational seminars, and more, all aimed at Black women. If you saw the hit 2017 movie *Girls' Trip*, starring Queen Latifah, Tiffany Haddish, Regina Hall, and Jada Pinkett Smith, you may have noted that the movie was set in a fictional version of the EssenceFest. In 2016, I was one of the honorees, among many others, at the "Empowered Brunch" hosted by vodka brand Cîroc and *Essence*.

At that time, Dia was working for a major business mogul. She had helped him seal a deal with spirits maker Diageo, bringing its marketing swagger to the once struggling Cîroc vodka brand. In 2015, Cîroc vodka reached sales of 2.6 million 9-liter cases, globally, up from 400,000 in 2009.

Dia is an accomplished executive and one that I wanted to add to my ecosystem of women whom I support and who support me—but it wasn't just her success and business acumen that earned my respect.

Dia's story doesn't begin with the glitz and glam of working with one of the world's most recognizable recording executives and tastemakers. She was born in Monterey, California. Her father was in the army, so the family moved in her younger years, first to Germany and then to Queens, New York, when she was six. The predominantly Black, middle-class neighborhood of East Elmhurst greatly influenced her. In her teen years, she recalls watching young people practicing dance moves in a nearby backyard. It didn't take long for what at first looked like a cool hobby or fun way to pass the time, to be featured regularly on music television station MTV. Two of the people in that backyard practicing were Cheryl James and Sandra Denton. You may know them as the vocalists in the barrier-breaking female rap group Salt-N-Pepa.

"I was able to watch, from a front-row seat, something that was like a cool, fun thing to do, become a full-on enterprise and become a global sensation before my eyes," she says.

If you suspect that this is where Dia made the decision to pursue a career in entertainment and marketing—and the rest was history— you're wrong. At this stage in her life, her intention was to achieve financial security through stable, reliable employment with the U.S. Department of Defense.

STARTING WITH INTENTION

We talk about intention, but how do we learn the importance of it? Earlier in this book, I shared how my father instilled intention in me and my sisters by asking us every morning: "What do you want to do? What do you want to be? Where do you want to go?"

Dia's father took a different approach. He decided she would go to a prestigious private school, St. Francis Prep, that would actively challenge his daughter's drive and intellect. His intention was so strong that he worked extra jobs and shifts to make it happen. After graduating from high school with high marks, she went off to college. Once finished with her undergraduate degree in psychology, she landed the job with the DOD.

In the years before Dia graduated, there had been a huge news story about defense overspending, revealing things like $500 hammers because there wasn't enough oversight. It was one of the biggest news stories of that time and a great embarrassment to the Defense Department and the US government as a whole. To improve the situation, the DOD put together a program to recruit and train high-performing young people who would take a better, more responsible approach to procurement.

The program was attractive to Dia because she was considering law school and the job would train her in contracts and negotiations. Getting into the program required interviewing with a panel of five high-ranking officials on a dais. Some candidates would be intimidated, but she leaned in fearlessly and was hired.

This is a point in Dia's life that I want to put special emphasis on. She went into the DOD program to learn and leverage. She became an expert in contract negotiations, a skill that—even though she didn't use it for a career in law—would impact her career in the future.

Dia completed her master's degree in business management while working, but as her role evolved, she no longer felt challenged.

"It was very slow, and they were literally giving me projects I would finish in a week that were due in four months." She knew she needed a change.

EMBRACING OPPORTUNITY

Many women don't change careers for fear of losing stability, staying in careers where they find themselves going through the motions. When part of your overall intention is to develop yourself and grow wealth, you can't be scared to change careers when it feels right. You also need to be cognizant of the amount of time you spend at any one stage of life when you still have more that you want to accomplish.

"I think, of course, when it comes down to risk-reward, my decisions come down to enormous respect for my time," Dia says. Like many of our most precious resources, time is often underappreciated. Dia's intentions to keep climbing, learning, and achieving were rooted in having respect for time.

It would be easy to stay in a job that you overperform in for stability, but is it contributing to your overall intention? Is fear preventing you from doing something new that could develop your skills and bring you closer to your vision sooner? How many years of enrichment and experience could you be losing by not swerving into that new path, even though the road may be a little bumpy at first?

Or maybe, like Dia, you're no longer feeling challenged. About that time, a friend suggested that she interview for a job in radio advertising sales. Her first reaction was a resounding *no*. She viewed sales as pushing things on someone. But her friend persisted, and Dia decided that interviewing wouldn't hurt.

"I was really just taking a chance. I wanted to get out of what I was doing at the Defense Department because I was getting bored with it," she says.

Was this the obvious choice for someone with an advanced degree and a DOD background? No, but it was a challenge and an opportunity to expand and diversify her network and learn new skills.

With this new job came a new payment structure, a draw salary that carries a lot of risk. For those of you unfamiliar with a draw salary, Dia explains it this way: "Basically let's say you agreed that the company will pay you $10,000 a month—you need to sell enough that your commission covers that $10,000 a month. Otherwise, you are in arrears and owe the company the difference. It was 'Eat what you kill.'"

Well, she killed it. But make no mistake—it wasn't easy. She took more from the job than a good paycheck. "It was hard, but I was able to do well, and it was actually the first time I realized that I could run a business," she says.

As much as she enjoyed the job, she was hungry for something more. With her newly developed entrepreneurial spirit, she started

Madison Marketing, an event and party promotion company, with a few friends in Washington, DC.

HUSTLE HARD

At Madison Marketing, Dia landed a deal to do work for Seagram's; the deal ranged from handling in-store and restaurant promotions to managing marketing activities at major sporting events. During this time, she began to see how running a business could provide both financial and personal rewards.

After the September 11 terrorist attacks in 2001, Dia decided that she wanted to move closer to her family again. She and her business associates wound down Madison Marketing, and she swerved into pharmaceutical sales for AstraZeneca, eventually going on to GlaxoSmithKline. She rose through the ranks and increased her wealth. Thoroughly enjoying her job in pharmaceutical sales, she recruited others she thought would be good at the job, and they too became top performers. Dia had developed an eye for talent, a critical skill for entrepreneurs, and now a new tool in her professional toolbox.

While Dia loved her job in pharmaceutical sales and was successful, she was pursued by a radio station to go back into radio sales. At first she refused, but then the general manager offered her such a great compensation package that she couldn't say no.

Dia was determined to make Bad Boy a client. She started at the radio station, and after the quick departure of a colleague, she received a flurry of accounts, one of which was Bad Boy Records. The Bad Boy account was a challenge. The record label's music executive refused to advertise at her station out of his loyalty to another station. Her breakthrough came when Bad Boy needed to do some promotion for New Edition. The R&B group appealed more to women, and her station played more of that kind of music than the station Bad Boy was loyal to. "I said, 'You know that doesn't make sense. You know we have more women listeners. If you're trying to sell records, this is the place to do it.' So the client agreed. That was the first time I got some advertising from them, and from there I got a piece of the Bad Boy records business on a regular basis."

SWERVING INTO BAD BOY RECORDS

Dia worked with the Bad Boy team for a year and then heard about a chief of staff position there. While some might want the job for the celebrity factor, this wasn't the case for Dia. She was most intrigued by what she felt she could learn from the Bad Boy CEO, considering that all his business would be under her purview. She interviewed for the position, and the company wanted to hire her, but for a different role, second executive assistant, since she hadn't managed big teams before.

Dia didn't scoff. Instead she said, "You can call me janitor, but this is how much I need to make." Dia asserted her worth and was willing to work her way up. Titles meant nothing so long as the experience to grow was there.

There's a major lesson here that everyone can learn from Dia—the art of being humble. She didn't have experience managing large teams, and instead of disputing it or walking away, she took the opportunity because she knew she'd learn what she needed to become chief of staff. She made it clear she needed to be paid a certain amount to do the job; she established and then didn't compromise her worth. People were telling her not to take the job for one reason or another, but she knew this was a path to something much bigger, so she quieted the voices and followed her intuition and intention and took the job.

Dia was promoted quickly at Bad Boy, probably due in part to her belief that you don't have to wait to make an impact . . . make an impact as early as you can because you get paid on day one.

She was promoted to senior executive assistant inside of three months, but still she had her eye on the prize, chief of staff.

She didn't always partake in the glitz and glamour of the job. She heard a story about a guy who was running one of his divisions who was close with the Bad Boy's CEO. The two were always traveling and socializing together. He was so close, in fact, that one day the CEO turned to him and asked, "Who's running my business, because you're always with me?" That story stuck with Dia.

Dia smiles as she talks about just how much work it was being the assistant for such a famous music tycoon. She would handle a wide range of things each day. In a day she could be working on record promotion while organizing birthday parties for his children. Her employer had a lot of homes, so she was often involved in his estate management. She worked with his team to make his travel schedule as efficient as possible.

> You don't have to wait to make an impact . . . make an impact as early as you can because you get paid on day one.

No matter what she was doing, talking to record execs or a landscaper, she held to her intention of "committing to excellence in each space."

ESTABLISHING YOUR WORTH

About two months into her promotion to senior executive assistant, Dia went to her boss with the original chief of staff job description and said, "I'm doing the role I initially interviewed for. What's it going to take to get the actual title change?" Again, she was following her intention and having a direct conversation about where she was, what she was giving the company, and what she had earned. He told her he'd think about it. Five days later they were meeting with Stephen Hill, at that time the head of BET, and Dia was introduced to Hill as her boss's chief of staff. In that subtle move, she was promoted.

"You know, I don't waste my time. I ran with it," she says, "That was that. That was my promotion."

Dia didn't just stop at chief of staff; again, she was looking at her next step and sticking with her initial intention. An opportunity came up with Diageo, one of the largest companies in the spirits industry. Dia wanted to be on the negotiation team, and her boss empowered her to go for it. The team negotiated a meaningful percentage of the profits for the spirits company Combs Wine & Spirits.

Dia tripled profits in the first 24 months, a phenomenal feat in the industry, partly as a result of helping to bring Cîroc vodka into the market (as mentioned earlier in the chapter). Dia says, "Cîroc vodka was an unexpected, tremendous success. It was a saturated market, so being able to come in with a small team and outdo what a multi-national multibillion-dollar company was not able to accomplish and sustain it to this day—I was enormously proud to be a part of it."

But getting to that point wasn't simple; she was still juggling her chief of staff duties and trying to build a brand that she estimated could become a $100 million business.

"I was on any given day still doing both (jobs). So it would be like booking the catering for the jet, making check-ins with the kids' schools, and then getting Cîroc into a major retailer and doing Diageo brand sessions. So I went to him, and I was just like, 'We have a huge opportunity here. I really do think that every part matters, but we have to prioritize what my focus is. We could build this $100 million business, or I could make sure there's apple juice on your plane.'"

For about three weeks it looked like her boss wasn't going to make the changes necessary for Dia to focus on building the spirits business, so she crafted a transition document and began packing her things. Then one day the company's chief financial officer came in and said her boss wanted to make it work. She was named president of Combs Enterprises, a new position.

Dia was the president of Combs Enterprises for a year. She had reached a goal that she had worked for years to achieve but recognized that she wanted more for herself. She desired a new challenge that would satisfy her entrepreneurial spirit. It was risky, but it was the intention that had evolved within her over time. Dia's path is a good example of how goals differ from intentions. She achieved many of the goals that she set for herself, but her intention was much bigger.

Dia elegantly transitioned out of the role at Combs Enterprises by putting together documents and presentations and providing training so that those left behind could pick up where she left off.

Why do this when leaving a job? It's part of nurturing your network, and it's a smart strategy. After all, you may need to call on someone at your old employer again.

Today Dia is the CEO of Lobos 1707 tequila and mezcal backed by a prestigious group of notables. No matter what risks she took or how many swerves she made—whether it was working for the U.S. government, working in pharmaceutical sales, or growing a spirits brand, Dia pursued them with an intention of excellence.

APPROACH LIFE LIKE DIA DOES

Do you see yourself in Dia's example, or do you think her approach to living an intentional life is right for you? If so, here are some tips to help guide you.

#1: Stay Focused on Your North Star

We've previously talked about the concept of a North Star, the ultimate intention that drives you. Throughout her career, Dia has been driven to pursue everything she touches with excellence. For her, it's tied to being able to call her own shots in her life.

"For me it's more about how I have freedom. How do I get to a level of financial freedom to make decisions that I want to make to be able to travel and to retire early?"

I'd be surprised if you aren't a lot like Dia. Many of us—men and women—we love our work, but ultimately we seek the financial freedom to control our destiny.

Having a balance between personal and financial fulfillment is important. Each propels the other forward. For instance, after all her years of hard work, one of Dia's greatest pleasures is deeply personal: reading to and cooking for her daughter. She takes the time to nourish her personal needs, and in doing that, she feeds her career side.

#2: Lift and Empower Other Women

A 2019 study showed that 17.6 percent of all board seats in the United States were held by women.[1] While that *is* a 3.4 percent increase from 2017 levels, it shows that women have a long way to go. As a woman who has worked in male-dominated industries, Dia is no stranger to being the only woman in the room. Through her career, she has worked to bring more women to the table. When she started at Combs Enterprises, there weren't many other women in leadership. "I brought on another five women executives," she recalls. "I was pretty intentional about making sure there were women represented in that company."

A male colleague once told her, "You brought in bad-ass female executives who made everybody better from a cultural standpoint and a financial standpoint," she recalls.

For Dia, supporting women means more than just bringing them in the door. She believes in advocating for them, whether that's making sure they aren't talked over in a meeting or that their ideas aren't dismissed. She seconds their opinions. She helps other women be heard at the table, not just get a seat there. She manifests her universal intention this way, not just working for herself but others.

#3: Keep Your Word

The more that I have come to know Dia, and call her a friend, the more abundantly clear it has become that she is a woman of her word. She honors her commitments. Her tolerance for risk, her desire for achievement, and her humility make her a force to be reckoned with.

"I have a resolution that I have made every year for like, golly, now maybe like 12 or 13 years," Dia says.

> "If I say yes, I will do what I say I'm going to do."

"And it is simple. I'm going to do what I say I'm going to do; that's it. It's not particularly exciting, but for me, it means learning. I continue to learn and evolve, and I'm not that great at saying no when I should say no, but if I say yes, I will do what I say I'm going to do. And to me, it's becoming a missing trait in the world, and I am proud I have it. Most people who ask about me will hear others say, 'If she says she's going to do it, you can go to sleep soundly. She's going to get it done.' I look for that same kind of trust with other people, and I hope that that's a hallmark of who I am."

3

FIGHT FOR YOUR RIGHT

Living on Your Own Terms

You'll learn, as you get older,
that rules are made to be broken.
Be bold enough to live life on your terms,
and never, ever apologize for it.
—MANDY HALE

Have you ever met people who seem like they've done some version of it all? Maybe they've lived and worked on several continents? Perhaps they've stepped away from traditional work to advocate for human rights or made that cause their life's work. Or possibly you've marveled at people who've taken career risks that you would never attempt. Often these people are living life on their own terms.

What is living on your own terms? I view it as having a life and career that is fulfilling and purpose filled. It doesn't necessarily have to be pursuit of a career. You could be passionate about traveling the world, keeping physically fit, or devouring diverse cuisines. It could be all these things! You can build the life you want at any time.

There will be forces, some benevolent, some well meaning, some less so, that will discourage you from turning the life of your dreams into a reality. Parents, friends, family, community, and society may pressure you to follow a "socially approved path."

Living life on your own terms may mean making choices that go against expectations and facing stigma, isolation, and uncertainty. It takes resolve and an unwavering belief in yourself to conquer that fear.

The act of living life on your own terms is something that I've admired in people whom I've worked with over the years. These are individuals who march to the beat of their own drum. When it comes to their career, they gravitate to the positions that are purpose driven, but also allow them the flexibility to do other things that bring them joy. Some would say that I would fall into this category given my approach to my personal and professional life. As much as I enjoy my purpose-driven career as a diversity practitioner, I have the flexibility to explore things that allow me to express my personal beliefs and my creative side, like being an activist, a writer, and a budding film producer. The freedom of being able to take charge and explore things that I enjoy allows me to live life on my own terms.

Living life on your own terms is at the intersection of intentionality. When you live life on your own terms, you move through life with few or no regrets because you've made it your business to live a life where there are no should-haves or would-haves in your vocabulary. That doesn't mean you won't have hiccups or that every move will be perfect, but at the end of the day, week, decade, you are likely to declare that you've had a life well lived.

Another woman who is making her own rules and living life on her own terms is broadcaster and entrepreneur Angela Yee.

MEET ANGELA YEE

Angela Yee is a radio personality best known for hosting *The Breakfast Club* morning show with her cohosts Charlamagne tha God and DJ Envy.

The Breakfast Club, which bills itself as "The World's Most Dangerous Morning Show," is syndicated to radio stations across the United States from its home at Power 105.1 FM in New York City and caters to a hip-hop audience. When you tune into the show, you're going to hear music by, interviews with, gossip about, and the hosts' opinions on the hottest stars including Cardi B and Drake.

Not to be limited by the show's focus on hip-hop, *The Breakfast Club* also attracts pop stars like Bruno Mars, comedians such as Chris

Rock, and actresses including Tracee Ellis Ross. Even legends such as Smokey Robinson have stepped up to the show's mic.

And if you think the show's focus is only on entertainment, let me disavow you of that. Savvy political strategists have recognized that the show's young, diverse audience—which at the end of 2020 numbered 4.5 million listeners each week—is a potentially influential and powerful voting bloc. Presidential candidates, including Vermont senator Bernie Sanders and former secretary of state Hillary Clinton as well as Joe Biden and Kamala Harris, have appeared on the show. I've even been honored to be a guest, to talk about careers and achievement and my first book, *Climb*.

If you spend a lot of time listening to radio shows, you may have noticed that women often are in the background. They tend to be supporting players to the men, sidekicks. Angela is not that kind of host, and *The Breakfast Club* isn't that kind of show. Angela, Envy, and Charlamagne get equal billing. No one cast member's name is in the show's title. Once you get to know Angela, you'll see why this show has been the right fit for her personality.

Angela's story begins in Flatbush, a Brooklyn neighborhood that a wide variety of people with roots in the Caribbean call home. Born to a Caribbean mother and Chinese father, she developed a tough skin quickly. Her dad was the only Chinese man in the neighborhood, so having the last name Yee meant having all the stereotypes and jokes that came with it flung at her, but she says that's what built those quick, snappy comeback skills, which would serve her later at the microphone.

"I didn't even have to think about race so much except for my last name. But I was cool with that. . . . I was never crying about it. . . . It was just jokes like, 'Oh, your dad knows karate,' stupid kid jokes. Nothing malicious," she recalls.

Her father's parents weren't happy about their son marrying a Black woman, so she and her older brother were often ignored by their grandparents. Some members of her father's family did embrace them, but this partial shunning robbed Angela of learning more about her Asian heritage. Almost everyone around her was Black. As a result, she identified more as Black than Asian from a very young age.

Angela's parents wanted her and her brother to have the best possible education and chance at life. They enrolled them in a program called Prep for Prep, which on top of their regular studies, required them to attend classes Monday through Friday for two summers, and then Wednesdays after school and Saturdays during the school year. Her world would change when she headed to Poly Prep in the seventh grade.

ADVOCATING FOR YOURSELF

Poly Prep was, by Angela's own admission, a tough adjustment for her. The school was private and academically rigorous, in keeping with her parents' plans for Angela and her brother. But it was also rich and very white, two things she was not used to. Despite the beautiful campus and opportunities Poly Prep could provide, Angela just wasn't comfortable there.

"They didn't do a great job of inclusivity, and there was a lot of racism at Poly," Angela recalls. "It did make me really uncomfortable, and it was hard for me. I lived in Flatbush. I was used to being in a school and in a neighborhood that was mostly Black students."

So began Angela's campaign to change schools. "It was an ongoing conversation with my parents. It was just me nagging them about it every day, me being extremely unhappy," she says. "Eventually they were like, 'OK.'"

A move to the New Jersey suburbs made her parents more amenable to the transfer, but her brother continued attending Poly while Angela enrolled in a diverse public school in New Jersey.

Looking back, Angela acknowledges Poly Prep wasn't all bad. "I do feel like being there helped me to navigate friendships with people of all different races," she says. "It's just understanding people as individuals rather than grouping them together. I think this is especially powerful with what is happening in the world now."

Angela cut class a lot, and that behavior landed her back at Poly Prep for her senior year. Upon graduation she went to college at Wesleyan University. Throughout her educational experience, teachers gave her good feedback on her writing, and that stayed with her. Her dream in college was to have a job that could fuel this passion.

"I had this goal, dream in my head, that I would be this artsy writer that would just get up, go to work, and then go home every day and write and not have anything to do with my nine-to-five and just focus on things for myself, but in reality, that didn't happen."

What did happen was a series of job and career changes that can only be described as Angela living life on her own terms. People who live life successfully on their own terms usually can do so because their intention includes working hard and exuding excellence—but also advocating for themselves when necessary. If a job or other situation goes left, they've put enough intention into their steps that they can often choose to go right. This is what I see in Angela's unorthodox path.

With the dream of a writer's life in her mind, Angela took a temp job doing data entry in a windowless office. The job turned out to be opening envelopes all day. After two days of misery, she quit.

Next up she had an interview at Columbia Records, but around the same time an opportunity arose to work as assistant to the CEO for the rap group Wu-Tang Clan, for whom she had interned previously. After talking to a trusted friend about the politics of working for a large record company (it was hard to learn and move up), Angela rejected the safer, more traditional corporate path by choosing Wu-Tang and worked with them for two years handling payroll and expenses, doing day-to-day office management, and coordinating with management and respective record labels.

Since members in the group were signed to numerous labels, this exposed Angela to people across the music industry. Her boss was busy and entrusted her with a lot.

"Everything kind of fell on me. It was a good situation. I would always be the first person in the office and the last one to leave," Angela says.

That led to a job with a prominent record label; she was back to something more traditional—and seemingly less risky. That didn't last. Angela got fired after refusing to do something that she didn't feel was right. But she was ready to pivot. She quickly joined a small urban marketing company doing work for clothing lines, mobile phone companies, and other clients. "I actually got hired the same day I got fired, because I already knew I didn't want to be there, so I had things set up," she recalls.

Things went well for a while. Angela was writing marketing proposals for the company, so she knew how much revenue it was bringing in, but her salary didn't measure up. The agency's owner would promise to pay her bonuses when a big check came in, but he never followed through.

That's when she brokered a deal with him to allow her to freelance. He agreed, and she began getting gigs with a range of clients. Her independent consultant star was rising. She even landed work with music industry royalty Nile Rodgers, who had worked with a range of artists including David Bowie, Madonna, and Diana Ross. Angela can't say for sure, but she thinks her boss wasn't happy with the success she was having without him. One day she went to the office and he yelled at her. "I have had an issue with people yelling at me ever since I was kid," she says. "So I took my laptop and never came back."

Her work as an independent consultant continued to grow. One of her former boss's clients reached out to her and asked if she would take him on as a client. Other people she had been collaborating with brought her into deals. She still had good relationships with members of Wu-Tang Clan and helped some of them with bookings and even managed affairs for founding member GZA during an overseas tour.

"I was doing management, all the while not having to work in an office and living life on my own terms," she recalls.

During this time, Angela nurtured a relationship that, unbeknown to her, would lead her to where she is now. Rapper Eminem was at the beginning of his ascension into rap royalty. Angela knew his manager, Paul Rosenberg, and she would send him boxes of clothes and hats for Eminem—clothing made by the company of a client. For a newer artist, this shows support and helps to validate the hard work the artist is doing to get noticed. For Angela's clothing company client, it was a win when people saw the rising rapper wearing the client's gear—especially when Eminem appeared on the cover of a magazine!

Eminem eventually launched a clothing line called Shady Limited, and Angela landed a job at its parent company, but like many clothing companies started by entertainers in that period, that didn't last long. She saw that there was a job opening in marketing at satellite radio company Sirius (which later combined with XM to create Sirius XM Radio), and she contacted Rosenberg to help her get an interview at Sirius where he and Eminem had recently launched Eminem's station Shade 45.

Things took an unexpected turn when Rosenberg asked Angela if she would consider an on-air job. It wasn't

> "My intention is always to do everything 110 percent."

something she had ever considered but, why not? She auditioned for the show, and for a couple of months the show continued to have her coming in, unpaid, to work.

"I was really, really bad at first, but I ended up getting a whole lot better just by grinding it out and getting more comfortable. Then we interviewed Jay-Z, and it went really, really well. They hired me right after the end of the interview," she says. Initially she was a sidekick, and then over the next few years got a morning show and added an evening show.

"Radio was never something that I thought I would be doing, but my intention is always to do everything 110 percent. That's the one thing I will say—for everything I've done, I give it my all. If you talk to anybody I have ever worked with or worked for, they'll tell you, 'Angela really works hard.' Some people will step on people to be successful. I chose to work hard to be successful instead, and it worked."

After a few years, Angela didn't see room for growth at Sirius. In 2010, she had a meeting with the program director at 105.1 FM in New York and was quietly told the station was putting together a new morning show lineup and wanted her to join Charlamagne and Envy. When she said yes, things moved quickly, as they often do when there's a major programming change in radio. Today *The Breakfast Club* is in over 100 markets and is aired on Revolt TV.

As Angela transitions into the next phase of her life, she's using the principles that have guided her, including being authentic, nurturing her network, and living her intention to work hard to move deeper into entrepreneurship. Those principles are being played out in one of her newer ventures. She was feeling run down and thought juicing might help. As she did more research, she realized some of what was being sold as healthy juices had a lot of added sugar, and she wanted to focus on whole fruits and vegetables. She opened a juice bar, Juices for Life BK, in Brooklyn in 2016 in partnership with rapper Styles P from hip-hop group The Lox. As of this writing, she has plans for a pressed juice business and a coffee shop.

LESSONS WORTH LEARNING

How can you navigate a path that includes living life on your own terms? Here are some lessons we can learn from Angela's experience.

#1: Work Hard, Be Professional, and Treat People with Respect

Angela's success at living life on her own terms didn't come by chance.

Even when she didn't know exactly what she wanted to do and was exploring her options, her work ethic didn't change. It also didn't change when her responsibilities meant being around celebrities, like the time she toured with Eminem and fellow rapper 50 Cent.

"Everybody that worked on the tour, to this day I'm still cool with them. I think people saw how professional I was. I was always on time. I was never in a bad mood. I was always polite to everybody, no matter what their position was," she says.

#2: Nurture Your Network

Angela's network has shown up for her repeatedly, from the friend who gave her the inside assessment of what it was like to work inside a record company, to Paul Rosenberg making the connection that helped her break into radio. She underscores how important it is to perform well when someone puts in a good word for you.

"You have to work even harder when somebody recommends you who you know, because it looks really bad if you don't deliver and that person put their neck on the line for you," she says.

You may recall that Angela emphasizes judging people not by their race, status level, or any other external factors and always being yourself. This also plays into being effective at building a valuable network. "Sometimes you don't know what your relationship with somebody is going to bring to the table at first," Angela says. "I have to be authentic, because it might be something that doesn't happen right away. It might be something that, five years from now, you're like, 'Thank God I know this person. They definitely put the good word in for me.'"

Last, networking can be fun—but it's not always. You should push yourself to do it regardless. Angela says, "I always tell people, 'Networking has the word "work" in it because it is still work.' There are times where maybe you don't feel like going out, times that you do feel like it, but you make yourself do certain things because you want to support a person that's been supportive to you, or just somebody that you're like, 'I like this person. I like what you're doing.' It means a lot to people."

Socializing can be a big part of networking. A lot of times when Angela goes out, it's work. "Maybe it's somebody having a celebration because they just got a promotion. I'll go out to that. Maybe it's somebody I've interacted with—I personally like them," she says. "I'll go and support somebody in that, and then make sure I congratulate them. Little things like that mean a lot to people. It means a lot when people do it for me."

#3: Insist on Your Worth

It's no surprise to anyone that women aren't paid as much as men. But women must insist on their worth. Sixty percent of women say they have never negotiated their salary, and only 34 percent of women negotiate salary offers, compared with 46 percent of men. Women are more likely to quit a job and find a new one than ask for a raise. However, negotiating your salary can yield an average 7.4 percent increase in a starting wage. But what happens when you negotiate an up-front agreement and your boss doesn't follow through? Remember what Angela did when she was working for the small marketing company. She pressed for better pay, and then when she didn't get it, she negotiated freelancing to bring in the money she knew she could earn. Then when that boss disrespected her, she walked. Knowing your worth financially, emotionally, and mentally—and demanding that people respect it—will serve you well. Don't forget that when Angela walked, she had options. When she faced an ethical quandary in a job and got fired for doing the right thing, she walked right into her next job.

4

THE COMPANY YOU KEEP

Strengthening Your Squad

There's one thing stronger than magic: sisterhood.
—ROBIN BENWAY

If you've ever heard the saying "Birds of a feather flock together," it's for good reason. It's common knowledge that we surround ourselves with people who are like us.

When you were a child, you likely had a circle of friends influenced by your family, school, and neighborhood. As you grew into adolescence, you took more control over your social circle, maybe with the goal to be more accepted or more popular. In adulthood, however, your world expands exponentially. The people you choose to spend your time with and energy on greatly affect your life, so it pays to be intentional about the people you let in.

I'm not alone in this belief. Countless studies do indeed reveal that our friends can influence our financial achievements, career performance, professional opportunities, and general life success.

Your closest friends can even have positive effects on your health and happiness. Our brains unconsciously absorb the vibe, if you will, of those around us. Humboldt State University social psychologist Amber Gaffney is quick to point out that it isn't imitation our brain processes, but something else. Imagine the brain saying, "I won't necessarily start copying you [the group], but I will change my attitudes to reflect your behavior because I feel similar to you and I see you as an extension of myself."[1] The question is, what do you want to reflect?

So let's talk about your squad—the people you keep closest. A squad generally is a group of people with the same task to carry out, but the word is more specifically associated with an athletic team or a small number of soldiers assigned to a specific mission. In these cases, members of a squad lean on one another to achieve success and support one another in their failures. In the military your squad members might be the difference between life and death.

Expressed another way, your squad consists of your ride-or-dies, the people you call first when you need advice and the ones you trust most. They aren't only those that help you; they also inspire you to achieve more personally and professionally.

High-achieving women have strong inner circles. Take, for instance, Tina Fey. This accomplished funny lady, author, actress, producer, and playwright keeps a strong squad including fellow actress, writer, director, and comedian Amy Poehler and actress, comedian, and singer Maya Rudolph. The women, who have all been *Saturday Night Live* cast members, have seen each other through good times and bad, created career opportunities, and lifted each other up. They also have an extended squad that includes other *SNL* female alums Rachel Dratch, Paula Pell, Emily Spivey, and Ana Gasteyer. These women not only work together but are rumored to have a group text chat where their conversations turn into content. Talk about #squadgoals.

When I considered who best to talk to about #squadgoals, I couldn't think of anyone better than Minyon Moore, whose squad includes political powerhouses Yolanda Caraway, Donna Brazile, Leah Daughtry, and Tina Flournoy.

MEET MINYON MOORE

Considered one of the most influential women in Washington, Minyon Moore is one of the nation's top strategic thinkers when it comes to political and corporate affairs and public policy. Among her many notable achievements, she served as assistant to the president and director of White House political affairs and public liaison for President Bill Clinton. In the Clinton administration she was a principal political advisor to the president, vice president, first lady, and senior White House staff. After leaving the White House, she went on to serve as chief operating officer of the Democratic National Committee. Since then, she's worked for Democratic public affairs firm Dewey Square Group, launched the first national African American women's political action committee, and served as an advisor for both of Hillary Clinton's presidential campaigns.

Minyon grew up in a working-class home on the South Side of Chicago in a family of four children. She was surrounded by community, and church was an important part of family life. Unfortunately, tragedy struck early in her life when her 13-year-old brother, Eugene, was hit by a train and killed. While devastated, she came away from the experience with a profound sense of empathy and wanting to help others. She channeled that pain into a lifelong intention of public service.

She found herself in the role of protector in her young life. Her younger brother, Carl, was often picked on in school, beat up by other boys in the neighborhood, and called "white boy" for being very fair-skinned.

"I learned to fight for him—and he tells this story all the time—because I felt like, you know, it was scarring him," she says.

She also spoke against injustice, no matter where it came from, including in the form of a bullying teacher who was picking on another student. Even when threatened with punishment, the young Minyon wouldn't back down until the teacher stopped. It's in these actions of a 10-year-old that we see the advocate emerge. Minyon set her intention early: There wouldn't be injustice on her watch.

But Minyon didn't always work in public service. For many years she had a successful career in advertising. During those years, drawn by its mission to effect social and civic change, she decided to volunteer for Chicago-based Operation PUSH, which today is known as the Rainbow PUSH Coalition. It wasn't an easy decision. "I started feeling this tug-of-war between me and my community. Do I serve my community? Do I continue to do what I'm doing?," she recalls. Rev. Willie Barrow, who cochaired PUSH with founder Rev. Jesse Jackson, encouraged her to make the shift. "She said, 'You need to quit that good-paying job,'" Minyon says.

It was the intention that she had set for herself early in life to fight for others, even when she wasn't aware that she had set it, that was her guide.

"I knew that I wanted to do something in the help-my-people category, but I wasn't really sure what that was. And so when I started volunteering, I really found out that I had so much joy in doing it, so much passion," Minyon says.

The job wasn't glamorous. Sometimes her role was to hold Reverend Barrow's purse. But she was in the room with Jackson and Barrow and some of the most powerful leaders in the country, and she was absorbing all the experience had to offer.

"I never pretended like I needed to be at the table. I just wanted to be in the room. But what it did for me was it sharpened who I was, and it caused me to have experiences that I didn't even know I would need to use until I became the person that was walking into the meetings on my own."

As Minyon became more involved in politics, her circle expanded. As with anything you're very involved in, certain people will repeatedly enter your orbit. This was the case as Yolanda Caraway, Donna Brazile, Tina Flournoy, and Leah Daughtry became part of Minyon's circle. You may be most familiar with Donna, a Democratic strategist who regularly appears on television news shows. Leah, also a political strategist, has served as CEO of two Democratic National Conventions. Yolanda has used her public relations and market expertise with numerous organizations, including the Democratic National Committee. Tina has served the Democratic Party in a number of ways, becoming chief of staff to Vice President Kamala Harris.

They became so close and their lives so intertwined that four of them—Minyon, Donna, Yolanda, and Leah—eventually wrote a book together (along with Veronica Chambers): *For Colored Girls Who Have Considered Politics*, which through their experiences working behind the scenes in politics provides a view of American history through the lens of their bond. Tina Flournoy didn't coauthor the book given that she had competing priorities regarding her time. Nonetheless, all these women are interconnected. No one is any more or less important than the other.

We've established the intention that Minyon set for herself to help others through her work. That led her to form the relationships that turned into a collective intention to support other sisters working as activists and strategists.

"One of the things I applaud in us is we have never seen each other as competition. In fact, we have always seen each other as a support system. When I have to do something, they rally behind me. When Donna has to do something, we rally around her. And that's how we have grown this friendship over the years," Minyon says.

The result of the 2000 presidential election was a crushing blow for the Democrats. Coming off the Clinton presidency there were high hopes that Vice President Al Gore would beat Texas governor George W. Bush and become the next president of the United States. Donna was Gore's campaign manager. The election ended with Gore conceding after a controversy involving a dispute over ballots in Florida. Broken down, bruised, and despondent, Brazile came to the DNC to work for Minyon, often acting as a gatekeeper—a role far below the one she had just completed. It was the opportunity and support she needed at the time, Minyon explains.

"What it did was cause her to get back involved," Minyon recalls.

The support that Minyon's squad, which she calls her "Sister Circle," has created runs counter to the negative narrative that is often promoted about women and is sometimes even supported by women.

In an article in *Harvard Business Review*, Mikaela Kiner, CEO of human resources consulting firm Reverb, writes about the omnipresent myth of female rivalry, or in her terminology, "Cycle of Female Rivalry," which she says "happens when a woman uses her power to keep another woman down, mistreats her, or competes unfairly."[2] There's this feeling that women have to dominate or topple other women to get ahead, to get the job, to get the man, to get the seat on the board. The big driver of this myth is the misguided belief that there is only "one seat at the table." It's a socially conditioned scarcity mindset and is also completely untrue.

> "You don't have to tear anybody down to build yourself up."

"I wish we lived in this perfect world where women understood the value, the collective value, of being in there together, supporting each other and understanding that there's plenty of room at the table or plenty of pie to get your piece and still support other women in getting theirs. You don't have to squeeze in that little slice," Minyon says. "You just expand the pie. You don't have to tear anybody down to build yourself up." Minyon's line is firm on women who are destructive toward other women, saying simply, "I have no tolerance for women who tear each other down." I would invite you to truly internalize her advice.

FIVE WAYS TO BUILD AND STRENGTHEN YOUR SQUAD

By now you know the importance of developing and nurturing your own squad. Now it's time to get down to the brass tacks—how to build and strengthen your squad. I've talked to a lot of women (and men) over the years and have always been fascinated with the people who have influenced them and the people they choose to spend time with. Based on years of anecdotal evidence, Minyon's advice and observations, and tons of research, I've put together five things you can do to build and strengthen your squad.

> "You have to build intentional relationships and not transactional relationships."

#1: Have Intentional Relationships and Not Transactional Ones

First let's define the difference between intentional relationships and transactional relationships, starting with the latter. Transactional relationships are more of the quid pro quo, this-for-that nature. These types of relationships rarely move past surface-level involvement because they are built on what people can do for you or you can do for them, and are sometimes singular or short term. Intentional relationships are active relationships that are nurtured and developed. They are deeper and tend to be longer term.

Minyon agrees: "You have to build intentional relationships and not transactional relationships. Many young women look at my relationship with Donna and others, and our circle is a bit bigger than others. They look at us and wonder how we do it and how we can stay this close. Then they get this notion that in a circle, someone will be jealous of them. Will somebody really want to support them? And so I say to them, 'My sister, is this your friend? Or is this an associate?' Exactly. What sphere, what lane do they sit in, because if it's really your friend, that friend is supporting you no matter what."

#2: Be Discerning and Selective

There's no way around it—you need a strong squad. However, strengthening your squad is not just about the people you invite in:

It's about those people you have to let go of as well. We have limited time to cultivate intentional relationships; we need to cut ties with people who no longer add value to our lives, and instead we need to identify the people who provide us with support and bring about opportunities. Creating and maintaining a squad is an intentional, ongoing practice. The more time you invest in fostering and nurturing positive relationships, the greater the benefits.

> "Raise your standards for your inner circle."

Do you want to be better? Surround yourself with better. You'll naturally rise to the occasion. If you are the average of the people you spend the most time with, consider what that means. World-renowned motivational speaker and self-betterment expert Tony Robbins sends a simple message: "Get rid of negative people who bring you down. Surround yourself with people who lift you up, lend you knowledge and help you learn from your mistakes. Raise your standards for your inner circle."[3] It's as much about the people you cut as the people you include.

#3: Change Your Mindset from Seeing Other Women as Rivals to Seeing Them as Sisters Instead

Be happy for other women when they rise. When women treat each other as rivals, it hurts our collective goals of equality in our personal and professional lives. When we join together, we collectively move forward and make more room for women to do well.

"I think a big part of it is seeing each other as sisters, instead of seeing each other as rivals," Minyon says. "And if we could change that mindset, things would be different."

#4: The Hardest Work Is the Work You Do on Yourself

Another piece of advice Minyon has for young women has to do with improving oneself. "I know that might sound cliché, but the hardest work you have to do is with yourself," Minyon says. "It is not with somebody you're competing with. It doesn't matter if you don't know who you are yet, but you need to have some fundamental understanding of what you will stand for and what you want. I promise you, even when you feel like you're competing, and remember that sometimes a little healthy competition is good, you'll feel good about where you are when you are working on you. Sometimes someone will get ahead of you and deserve to, and knowing that will help you be better. Working on yourself is for life." Of course, it's most important to do this for yourself, but you do have to remember that part of building a strong squad means being a valued member as well. To attract the right people, you need to be what you are looking for in a close confidant.

> "You need to have some fundamental understanding of what you will stand for and what you want."

#5: Find a Mentor or Coach to Guide You

This final piece of advice is critical and something to take to heart. A mentor or coach is a crucial part of your squad. Why? Because this person not only is going to guide you, but is also going to give it to you straight. Your mentor or coach not only will celebrate your victories with you, but will also help you do a postmortem on each failure to make sure you get the most out of each experience, even when you'd rather just ignore it and forget.

I asked Minyon that if she were part of a young millennial woman's squad, what is the best advice she could give herself. Her response: "Keep getting back up. All of us have failed at something, and we just get back up. If you fail, is it going to destroy your life? No, it's just a set-back. This is why it's imperative to have good mentors around you, because when you fail, you need people who will offer you encour-agement, who will pray with you and let you cry for a minute. But then they'll say, 'OK, girl. Let's work it out now; let's get up.' We all need somebody that we can pour into when we fail. But we need somebody that can pull us back up, too."

> "Keep getting back up. All of us have failed at something, and we just get back up."

5

STRONG MINDS

Avoiding Fallout from Burnout

I am enough.
—UNKNOWN

If you are reading this book, chances are you hold yourself to a high standard. You may even say you're a perfectionist and feel proud of yourself for commanding yourself to live your #bestlife. Great, right? Perfectionism can indicate a healthy drive to excel, but only if you are able to forgive yourself when mistakes happen and do not obsess over everything being just right.

But you have to ask yourself—are you obsessed with being perfect? Are you able to forgive yourself? Are you able to stop before you burn out? If you're like most women, you likely struggle with perfectionism.

WHAT IS PERFECTIONISM?

Unfortunately, many of us don't just let our missteps go, and many of us have an unhealthy focus on being the best all the time; no sick days, no bad days, and no excuses. It's this compulsion that, if not channeled properly, can veer into toxic behavior and environments. So what's the difference between high standards and perfectionism? *Psychology Today* says, "Perfectionists set unrealistically high expectations for themselves and others. They are quick to find fault and overly critical of mistakes. They tend to procrastinate a project out of their fear of failure. They shrug off compliments and forget to celebrate their success. Instead, they look to specific people in their life for approval and validation."[1]

Competition, whether it's in the workplace, in school, or in life in general (especially on social media), drives this incessant need to be perfect. In their 2019 article "Perfectionism Is Increasing over Time: A Meta-Analysis of Birth Cohort Differences from 1989 to 2016," researchers Thomas Curran and Andrew P. Hill found that self-oriented perfectionism increased by 10 percent, socially prescribed perfectionism increased by 33 percent, and other-oriented perfectionism increased by 16 percent in the millennial population.[2]

Now that's not to say that perfectionism is all bad. Perfectionism has helped me excel, though I am sure that it has also hindered me in some ways. Perfectionism might cause individuals to lose sight of the overall objective, overanalyze, and miss deadlines. Many often struggle with it, but I choose to lean into it. There are a lot more pros than cons to perfectionism. You will generally do things well, and you'll be perceived as someone who can get things done! You are driven and motivated to give your best in everything that you do. I choose to harness the positives of perfectionism.

Millennial women are in a unique circumstance when it comes to perfectionism. All eyes are on women to catapult the women's movement further ahead. There's pressure to be leaders, inventors, C-suite executives, entrepreneurs, mothers, mountain climbers, and do it all at the same time. Millennial women of color, in particular, not only feel the pressure of the women's movement but also deal with the legacy of centuries of systemic racism. They do it all while fielding microaggressions and, let's face it, aggressions that aren't so micro. It's a burden that should not have to be carried but sadly still exists.

TOXIC WORK CULTURE: WHERE PERFECTIONISM, BURNOUT, AND HEALTH ISSUES MEET

While perfectionism takes root in all areas of our lives, our professional arena can seem like the one we have the least control over. Toxicity in the workplace, where people are overworked and underappreciated rather than being nurtured and encouraged to work to their fullest potential, is a challenge for some organizations. Examples of toxicity in the workplace can include exclusionary work environments and cultures, poor leadership, stifled career growth opportunities, and passive-aggressive communication styles, among others. Toxic work cultures take a toll on one's confidence and health, not to mention bleeding into one's personal life.

The dangers of toxic work culture are far-reaching. In the *Inc.* magazine article "4 Devastating Consequences of a Toxic Workplace Culture," Tanya Prive lays out ways a toxic work culture hurts companies. One, in particular, is felt by both employee and employer: an increase in illness and absenteeism due to—you guessed it—burnout.[3] Not only does that mean your personal health is at risk, which, let's keep things in perspective, is the most important consideration. But increased absenteeism may also mean a loss of opportunity or an undeserved reputation for being unreliable or less "adaptable" to the environment than colleagues not experiencing burnout.

There's no greater partner for perfectionism than burnout; they seem to go hand in hand. Workers nationwide are feeling the pressure to be available at all times. This became even more evident in the early days of the COVID-19 pandemic. According to a survey of 1,099 US workers conducted in April 2020 by the Society for Human Resource Management, 41 percent of employees said they felt burned out from their work, 45 percent said they felt emotionally drained from their work, and 44 percent said they felt "used up at the end of their workday."[4] But is everyone feeling this in the same way? Not so!

Women, in particular, were maxing out and burning out during the COVID-19 crisis, the result of their taking on more housework and caregiving responsibilities than men, Facebook chief operating officer Sheryl Sandberg and her LeanIn.org cofounder, Rachel Thomas, wrote in a *Fortune* op-ed published in May 2020. Women are also more likely than men to report experiencing sleep issues and physical symptoms of severe anxiety, according to LeanIn.org and SurveyMonkey research.[5] So this leaves the question, how can women become successful and follow their intention, no matter how big, without falling prey to the dark side of perfectionism and burnout? For answers, I thought of no one better to turn to for advice than Davia Temin.

MEET DAVIA TEMIN

Davia Temin is in the business of fixing toxic work environments. She is the founder, president, and CEO of Temin and Company, a boutique management consultancy focused on international crisis, reputation, corporate governance, thought leadership, and risk management, with a specialty in cybersecurity, sexual harassment, and the securities industry.

> "I have this belief:
> If you're going to
> do something, overdo it."

It's wide-ranging work, typically crossing international borders and confidential in nature. Temin and Company's work has included putting together and executing a strategy to withdraw a popular drug from the market and then successfully reintroduce it to the market after a healthcare crisis; being on point in plane crashes, oil spills, and global cyberattacks; and advising boards when their CEOs have misbehaved and have needed to be replaced, such as in #MeToo-related instances. Her team coaches CEOs, corporate boards, and leaders in academia and advises clients on a range of tough, strategic issues. Essentially, Davia helps people and organizations get past challenges and shore up their reputations so they can focus on the business of doing business. She's also a self-described perfectionist who has learned how to channel the trait successfully.

Her work requires having a broad view of the world. Davia was raised in Cleveland, Ohio, the only child of older parents. She grew up feeling more like an adult than a child as a result, which she found stimulating and instructive. Her father was an electrical engineer and had clients all over the world from diverse backgrounds. It wasn't unusual for Davia to meet her father's clients and have dinner with them. This expanded her young worldview far beyond Ohio's borders and instilled in her what she terms a "global love."

"I got to be friends with all of these people from around the world and who I felt perfectly comfortable with," she says. "I didn't feel like a kid. . . . [the people] I met were the broadest range of people you can ever imagine. My father reveled in diversity. I mean, he just reveled in it."

Being more like an adult than a child, she also leaned into perfectionism young as a Girl Scout, selling more Girl Scout cookies than any other girl in Ohio in her year, explaining, "I have this belief: If you're going to do something, overdo it." That same perfectionism now manifests itself in her work in how she drives herself and her team. "If you're going to do something, do it in an A-plus-plus-plus-plus way," she says. "Sometimes when I say this . . . folks in my company say, 'Take off a couple of pluses, please. This is a lot of pressure.' And I go, 'No, no; if we're going to do it, we're going to do it really, really, really, really well.'"

Davia maneuvered through numerous twists and turns before the intention that guides her life and work took shape. She had many interests, among them physics and dress designing, and was pulled in several directions, always wanting to do many things at once, something she jokingly refers to as repeating identity crises. Along the way, she started Columbia Business School's magazine, and almost moved

63

to Paris to write an art history dissertation on how Edgar Degas framed the ballerinas in his paintings. Eventually—through her time at Columbia as head of public affairs, sitting in on classes—she realized she had an interest in commerce and took a job launching the marketing function for a global investment bank.

That's when Davia decided to go all out for success. She rose and rose in the corporate world, but along the way, something didn't feel quite right. She began to witness some of the characteristics of toxic work environments—many people were mean, unhealthily competitive, or without any purpose beyond making money. While she found she loved the world of business, she also felt strongly that it needed to be balanced by a sense of kindness, caring, and purpose. Without those elements, success just felt empty.

It was an experience with the Dalai Lama—yes, the Dalai Lama—that offered some clarity to her. She almost didn't go to see the Dalai Lama speak at a church in New York City. It was a $500 ticket, too expensive for her at the time, but a friend involved with the event offered to put her on the list. The Dalai Lama spoke about compassion on a global level and then opened up the room for questions, and people started to line up, asking question after question. Davia's was burning inside her, and right as it was about to be her turn, two large men stood on either side of her and said the Q&A was ending and she wouldn't be able to ask her question. She sat down still consumed by what she had wanted to ask. Davia discovered that in all her success, she had lost something really important to her, compassion.

Then in a serendipitous turn of events, although the Dalai Lama was due to go to a dinner, he stayed for the reception afterward, and she could see him across the room eating, of all things, what looked like Doritos. It's as though his complete humanness was on display, and he connected with Davia.

She recounts: "He's looking at me from afar. All of a sudden he starts walking. He walks directly to me, and he stops in front of me, and I'm holding my hands out. And he takes hold of my hands. He's looking straight into my eyes, cocks his head, and says, 'So, so?' Of course, I start to cry, and my question tumbles out, 'Can someone who has lost their compassion, or never had it to begin with, regain it?'"

He indicated that a person could, and then he elaborated: "In Buddhism, we say that the Buddha is within every person. And you can look into the eyes of your torturer as he is torturing you. And you can see the Buddha within him. Similarly, the Buddha is always within you, whether you know this or not. And you can always find him whenever you wish." When he said those words, something registered deep within her. She realized she was really asking about redemption, and in his answer she saw a better way forward. That's the moment when Davia stopped focusing only on success and instead made an intention to build a life and work around kindness and integrity, making it her purpose to help resolve crises with integrity, kindness, and compassion for all sides.

MAKING AN INTENTION TO LIVE WITH INTEGRITY

What Davia experienced in the corporate environment influenced her desire to build a company that would have integrity as its core value.

"I learned through all the years in corporate life that they say one thing when they hire you: 'We want you to come in and be a disruptor. We've never had a marketing organization. We've never been marketing centric. We want to break those barriers. We want you to tear them down and rebuild them,'" she explains. "But in reality that is not always the case. Mostly, in my experience, they really didn't want you to do much but talk a lot about it."

When Davia considered what her intention was, what her greater purpose was, she realized that she had to build it herself, because integrity was at the crux of her intention.

"I wanted to build my own company with layers of integrity, because in crisis management, what happens is when the pain is great enough, a company or an organization or an individual will almost do anything to make the pain stop. And often those things do not have integrity, or they're not ethically or morally based," she says. She knew that the forfeiture of integrity would mean that things could be achieved faster and easier. But she also knew that if she could not stay true to her North Star, she would not be building something she could be proud of, or even a part of. Her intention led her to build a firm in the only image she could fathom. "I wanted to create a firm that was quite the opposite, that would use integrity to create the right solutions for a crisis. Long-term, good solutions for a crisis create the right kind of response and apology, the right kind of thought leadership and intellectual leadership, the right kind of governance and competition, and the right ways to get beyond the crisis," she says. "It's like a refiner's fire: If you walk through it in the right way, you can come out stronger and finer and better, not morally challenged, but with more resolve. And so that's sort of the ethos of how I built the company. It's the ethos of how I do the coaching."

> "If you have a grander purpose, intention is what gets you there."

In my observation of Davia—and when listening to her speak—I have been particularly struck with the way intention with integrity is akin to a philosophy of living for her. She explained intention to me, saying, "I think it is very, very aligned to purpose. So if you have a grander purpose, intention is what gets you there. Intention is what gets you over the finish line. Intention is what gets you to do the right thing. Intention is what gets you to do the good thing. Intention is what fuels a life of purpose. Intention is a guide for how we live our lives." This is again where we see just how different having an intention and having a goal is—intention is almost divine in its providence and makes a life of meaning.

DAVIA'S TIPS FOR CREATING
A POSITIVE PROFESSIONAL LIFE

Women, especially younger women, are highly vulnerable in toxic corporate cultures since retaliation and blowback for reporting bad behavior are very real threats. With this in mind, there were several insights Davia shared with me that I believe can help millennial women navigate their professional lives.

#1: Get Perspective

Your colleagues will have their own opinion of you when you're outside of the room, and you can't control that, Davia says. However, when you are inside the room, it's another experience altogether. She advises, "You'd better have a sense of humor and think carefully through what is acceptable to you, what is not acceptable to you, and what you can pass off with some humor."

You also need to understand that, ultimately, this is work and everyone isn't there to make you happy and help you achieve. You're at work to grow the company and, the hope is, align with its mission. If you find the mission is in opposition with your intention or values, it's unlikely the company will change it for you, and you may need to find another job. If you're 60–40 on the mission, maybe you can live with it. You need to manage your expectations of the company and of yourself.

#2: Have a Support System

We've talked in past chapters about the importance of having a support system. This is a trusted group of people you can bounce ideas off or just relax with. Look for support system candidates in your workplace, place of worship, alumni organizations, or friend groups. Having a support system reduces isolation and loneliness, allows you to respond better in times of crises, and helps you maintain better health.

#3: Learn and Understand the Unwritten "Rules"

When we talk about privilege, one element of privilege is knowing the unwritten rules of society and leveraging them to be successful. However, when you aren't born into that knowledge, you have to seek it out. This may not be a very popular tip, but there's definitely still a "look" to getting the position.

"I know you want to dress the way you want to dress, and you want to be who you want to be. But understand, as you are climbing the ladder, what you did one time may not get you there the next time," Davia says. "Every time you go up a rung, you have to grow. I mean, you have to change, you have to cut your hair, or you have to wear different clothes. You have to learn how to speak differently. You have to do whatever it might be. You have to meet those mores that you see at those levels, not the noxious ones, not the stupid ones, or the snide ones, or the awful ones, but the ones that are just the culture."

In some industries, you can absolutely have rainbow-hued hair—say, in the beauty, music, or fashion industry—and it won't inhibit your upward mobility. However, in a more historically traditional environment like financial management, it may hold you back. Is it right? No. Is this the way it is, at least for now? Yes. These are the unwritten rules, and the sooner you learn them for your chosen field, the faster you'll rise.

#4: Have a Properly Planned Exit Strategy and Only Use It When You Really Need To

There's a reason why people say not to burn your bridges; you'll likely need them one day, and in this very social world we live in, your potential new employer may know your old one. That's why choosing to leave a position should not be haphazardly decided or executed. The best reason to leave a job is to level up somewhere else with promotion and increased compensation. Sometimes a job isn't a good fit, or there is a toxic work environment. No matter the reason, plan a graceful exit. Before leaving, find out if the company will pay out unused sick or vacation time. Make a plan to return any equipment that needs to be returned to the company. If you utilize the company insurance and 401(k) plan, be sure you have a plan for your transition.

Once you have your game plan together, tell your supervisor first and give the customary two weeks' notice. Some companies will let you (or ask you to) leave the same day, and others will accept the notice. If you work out the two weeks, stay on top of all your responsibilities and keep acting like the consummate professional you are—in essence, act like you are still working there! Follow all protocols, and don't take long lunches or skip meetings unless you are asked not to attend. When it is time to do your exit interview, be honest but diplomatic. If there are systemic issues you feel need to be pointed out, write them down in advance to be sure you express yourself positively and constructively. Ideally, you want to leave on the best terms possible.

THREE TIPS FOR DETOXING YOUR PERSONAL LIFE

I'd be remiss if I only mentioned ways to create balance in your professional life without talking about your personal life. We are just as prone to perfectionism and burnout there, too! I've put together three tips for doing a simple but effective detox for your personal life if you are feeling a little run-down, maybe a bit uninspired, or just off track.

#1: Revisit Your Intention

In our day-to-day hustle, we can lose focus of our intention for our lives. Endless to-do lists, boxes to check, kids to get to soccer, and "just one more email" to answer turns 7 a.m. into 11 p.m., and you're headed to bed and wondering where your day went. We've all been there. And here's the truth: We'll all be there again. But take an hour or two and block it out on your calendar. Sit down with your journal, a clear mind, and a cup of tea or glass of wine, and write down your intention. Be as specific as you can. Now consider the following questions:

- Am I getting closer to or further from my intention each day?
- What would I like to bring into fruition in a smaller sense?
- What would I like to bring into fruition in a large sense?
- What can I do to bring attention to my intention each day?

Reflect on your answers, and find ways to incorporate intention into your day every day.

#2: Evaluate Your Stress

Similar to what you did in the first exercise, evaluate your stress level. You can evaluate your stress as a whole or evaluate it in categories like "work," "home," "health," etc. Ask yourself questions like:

- Where do I have the most stress?
- What's causing my stress?
- How much of my stress is bad stress? How much is good (motivating) stress?
- Do I secretly like being stressed? Do I think it makes me feel accomplished or needed?
- Am I experiencing health issues—physical or mental—due to stress? If so, what kinds?

- What stressors do I have control over?
- What sorts of things can I do right now to reduce stress levels?

#3: Assemble Resources (and Use Them!)

Now that you've taken a pulse regarding your stress, it's time to do something about it. There are many ways to relieve stress or redirect it into positive spheres. Here are a few things that have been widely found successful in reducing stress:

- Therapy with a trained counselor, therapist, or doctor
- Health and wellness podcasts
- Ted Talks
- Meditation, breathing apps like Calm and Headspace
- Exercise
- Yoga/mindful movement
- Meditation
- Journaling
- Art or another creative outlet
- Volunteering
- Communing with nature

• • •

Regularly practicing one or any combination of these self-care methods will improve your personal life. Cultivating grounding personal habits will inevitably spill over into your professional life, giving you more energy, better focus, and a stronger mind. So set your intention to climb to the highest rung of any ladder; just don't forget to take the necessary steps to avoid fallout from burnout while you do it.

6

LIFE COACHES

Adopting a Holistic Approach

Success is not final; failure is not fatal;
it is the courage to continue that counts.
—WINSTON CHURCHILL

Have you ever wondered why people hire life coaches? I mean, how can you be coached on something so broad as life? Well, I am here to tell you that life coaches, when you find the right one, can help you develop all areas of your professional and personal life. Have I sipped the life coach Kool-Aid? You bet! Let me tell you: It tastes great!

A life coach fulfills a different role in a successful woman's life than those of others in her entourage. A life coach is not the same as a therapist. A therapist is someone who looks at your past to help you understand why you are the way you are. Nor is a life coach a mentor, someone who offers advice based on her experiences. A life coach helps you tap your full potential, defining who you want to be and what you want to accomplish. Unlike many consultants who propose a solution and leave you to your own resolve, a life coach stays with you to help you integrate changes, new skills, and goals to make sure you follow through. Life coaches offer new perspectives and challenges that honor your intentions so that you can live your best life.

As you think about your intention and the goals you'll need to achieve to get there, a life coach may be able to help you along the way. Whether you get stuck, encounter an obstacle, or experience a failure—or even if you just need an accountability partner—a life coach can help get you, or keep you, on track.

In this chapter, we're going to hear from successful life coach Marie Forleo and get her insights and even some "free advice" to get you thinking. We're also going to learn when and how to use the services of a life coach to take your personal life, professional career, or business venture to the next level. I'll also give you a few helpful hints on how to choose a life coach who meshes best with you.

> "Everything is figureoutable."

MEET MARIE FORLEO

Entrepreneur, writer, philanthropist, and self-proclaimed unshakable optimist, Marie Forleo is just the person you want in your corner. Her company has been recognized in *Inc.* magazine as one of the fastest-growing women-led private companies in America. She's worked with business magnate Sir Richard Branson, whose empire spans travel, leisure, entertainment, space, and more; renowned broadcaster, producer, actress, and author Oprah Winfrey; Tony Robbins, the sought-after speaker and coach; and everyday people. She reaches her audience with her award-winning show *MarieTV*, online training programs, and books including *Everything Is Figureoutable.*[1]

Marie was born and raised in New Jersey. Her parents divorced when she was an adolescent, and Marie lived with her mother, a big influence in Marie's life and work. It's her driven, hardworking mother that gave her the signature phrase that became the title of her book, "everything is figureoutable."

"I was brought up with this notion that if you have a dream and work hard, you can create a way to a better life. I think all those ingredients helped form who I am as an adult," Marie says.

This belief powers her role as a personal coach. "When I look at people, I see their potential, and I look for their gifts. I believe in their intrinsic value and capability to transform or transcend any circumstance that they face." This inimitable spirit is what eventually led her to becoming a life coach, but not without getting a lot of experience and doing a lot of soul-searching.

WHEN THE "DREAM JOB" ISN'T YOUR DREAM

Certain jobs are widely accepted as "dream jobs," like working at internet search and advertising giant Google, at fashion's bible *Vogue*, or for TV and film trailblazer Oprah. But what happens when you get one of those jobs and it's just not your dream? Do you suck it up and push on, thinking it's some sort of flaw in you and not an indicator that maybe there's no such thing as a universal dream job? Marie found herself in this exact space. She was working on Wall Street as a trading assistant on the floor of the New York Stock Exchange. It was a prestigious role, as accepted by society. She felt like she was stuck in a dream job that seemed more like a nightmare.

> "I believe in their intrinsic value and capability to transform or transcend any circumstance."

Working on Wall Street was fulfilling a need; she had to do well financially. It wasn't that she valued material things. Marie had seen her parents get divorced over financial difficulties. She made the connection early that money problems could damage love. She recalls a conversation with her mother where she implored her daughter never to let a man control her money or her life.

"It was like one of those imprinting emotional moments that I will never forget," Marie says. "And I made myself a promise that day. I said, 'When I grow up, I vow to find a way to make enough money that it'll never cause this kind of stress again.'"

But years later, surrounded by men making money hand over fist (and then often heading to the strip clubs after work), she realized that money wasn't a key to happiness.

"All these guys I'm working with, they were making a gajillion dollars. From my perspective, I'd never even heard of this much money in my life yet. All of them, even though they were rich financially, they seemed spiritually bankrupt. They were pining for these two weeks out of the year where they could be on vacation, and otherwise, based on their behavior, it did not seem like they were very happy with their lives," she recalls.

She struggled with what to do and remembers thinking: "Marie, this isn't who you are. This isn't what you're meant to do. This isn't who you're supposed to be in the world. That small voice inside kept speaking up, but it wasn't telling me what I was supposed to do instead. And based on my upbringing, my parents worked hard to put me through college, how could I quit this job? I didn't know what I was supposed to do instead, even though every day, it felt like I was dying a slow death. So one day I showed up for work, something like six or eight months into the gig, and I started having what I can only identify now as a panic attack on the floor."

Marie turned to her father for advice, and he said something that surprised her because it wasn't, "Suck it up, kid," or "I paid all this money for you to go to school and get a job like this." He said something far more nuanced and true: "You're going to be working for the next 40 to 50 years. You have got to find something you love. If this job is making you this sick and you've been doing it for eight months, you need to quit and go find something that you love. However long it takes you to find, that's just how long it's going to take you. But once that all locks into place, life is going to work, but you cannot just chase the money. You have to find something you love." With his words in her mind, Marie left the New York Stock Exchange without regret and was no longer plagued by the guilt of leaving a so-called dream job.

Marie eventually found herself at Condé Nast, working for fashion and beauty magazine *Mademoiselle*, another "dream job," but she still hadn't found her place or purpose. This time she ran across an article about life coaching—which was still quite new—and was intrigued. She signed up for a three-year, teleclass-based life coach training program. She worked at the magazine during the day and did her coaching studies on nights and weekends. About six months later, she was selected for yet another dream job. "I got a call from the HR department at Condé Nast. They had a promotion for me. I could go to *Vogue* with more money, more prestige, and an actual career that people could understand and sounded impressive," Marie recalls. But she didn't jump at the offer. Instead she thought about life coaching. She could take a pass on *Vogue* and pursue life coach-ing, which would have the prestige of no paycheck or health benefits. No one even really knew what it was at the time. Marie decided to push past her fear of moving into a new career direction and took action.

> "Intention for me is something that you can embrace right now, and it's about energy."

"My heart told me that it was time to leave the corporate world and just give this thing a go. I quit my stable job. I went back to bar-tending and waiting tables, which is how I helped put myself through college. I started my life coaching business, and that was 20 years ago." As it turns out, her heart was right all along. She overcame her fear of failure, of not being experienced enough, and most of all, she took a chance on herself.

SUCCESS BEGINS WITH INTENTION

As you know, intention is a critical part of success, as we've learned in past chapters, and it's especially meaningful when we talk about decid-ing to work with a life coach. Marie gave me some insight on how she distinguishes goals from intention; she talks about intention as a living thing. Marie explains: "I feel like setting a goal is very specific, narrow, and outcome-oriented. It's clear, it's time-bound, and it's in the future, right? It's something that you're aiming toward that likely is not going to happen in this particular moment. Intention for me is something that you can embrace right now, and it's about energy. It feels more open, more flexible and fluid. It's about influencing an outcome, but more about the energy with which you're doing something, rather than it has to be the specific narrow thing that either you hit or you don't."

Before hiring a life coach, it's important to take some time to think about your intention. What type of life are you hoping to manifest? What energy, like Marie says, are you looking to both project and embrace? You don't have to know everything. You don't have to draw out the map or get the "how-to" together, but get a good feel for your intention before starting the process of looking for a life coach. It will help you articulate what you desire and find the best coach to help you fulfill your intention.

MARIE'S APPROACH TO COACHING:
THE GUIDE ON THE SIDE

Marie's approach to coaching is rooted in the belief that much of the power lies within the clients themselves. She says, "I believe in my soul that any people that I work with, they are their wisest teacher. They have the answers within them."

Marie sees her role as being her clients' partner in helping them access that wisdom, knowledge, and internal intelligence they already possess. Marie also helps them to create action steps and strategies for moving. Her philosophy positions her as a sounding board and place of support for her clients, all in the name of helping them realize their intention.

Marie calls her role in the process the "Guide on the Side," helping usher her clients to their next big thing through their own unique gifts, intuition, and knowledge. She is not all-knowing, nor does she want to be, saying, "I don't have all the answers. I'm no 'Sage on the Stage.' I'm more of a 'Guide on the Side,' but I know you have all the wisdom inside. I'm here to partner with you to pull that out, and I can help you create anything you really want. But it's up to you to tell me what that is."

If you consider hiring a life coach, you should be clear that a life coach is not a therapist. Life coaching is all about the person you are now and where you're going. It's asking and answering the question, "Who do you want to be?"

So let me ask you, "Who do you want to be? What do you want in your life? Do you need help getting there?" If you do, a life coach is an ideal resource.

WHO NEEDS A LIFE COACH?

Does everyone need a life coach? In his *Entrepreneur* article, "Why Everyone Needs a Life Coach," Luis Garcia, the founder and CEO of Red Wolf Entertainment, a public relations and marketing firm that counts NBC Universal, BMW, and Rolls Royce among its clients, argues that those who want to be successful do.

He says, "Living your best personal and professional life requires intentional self-reflection and continual personal development. Even at our best, however, we all have blind spots that prevent us from seeing the whole picture of our lives and the thoughts, habits, and behaviors that hinder our growth."[2]

Why can't we just turn to our best friends and trusted family members? They have blind spots too! He goes on to say, "While loved ones may have the best intentions, they often lack the discernment to appropriately analyze and deliver actionable advice. So, who do we turn to for unbiased evaluation and expertise? Enter the life coach."

A life coach not only has the ability to mirror yourself back to you, but can also help you identify the blind spots that may be holding you back, encourage you to open your mind, and support you as you make the sometimes-scary moves that can shake even the strongest of us. There are lots of reasons to work with a life coach, some professional, some personal, and some that intersect in both spheres.

> You have to be able to articulate what it is you want.

"People often stumble upon my work online after finding themselves in some type of transition, in a challenging place where maybe they're feeling a bit depressed, they're feeling a bit lost or confused, they've had some type of big rejection or disappointment, or they've had a life change where things don't feel as clear as they used to," Marie says. Of course, some people want to work with a life coach to start a new business, get healthier, level up in their career, or find a partner— anything they want to accomplish.

However, there is one key to being able to work successfully with a life coach—you have to be able to articulate what it is you want, which is often easier said than done. Marie recognizes this difficulty, saying: "I think that so many of us are not taught how to really clarify and articulate our own dreams and goals. And I don't think many of us are taught to explore or define what success feels like and looks like for ourselves." For many people, their dreams aren't really their own. They've simply absorbed society's and their family's ideas of what they should want. Marie advises her clients to ask themselves what success is to them at this stage of their life, fully remembering that their intention will grow and change and evolve as the years go on. When considering hiring a life coach, you should first get your arms around answering one question for yourself: "What do I want to do, or where do I need help?" From there, you'll be able to start the selection process.

Choosing a life coach is like picking any other valued member of your support team and should be done carefully. Unfortunately, unlike for therapists and other professionals, no governing body is setting industry standards and offering certifications. You'll need to vet prospective coaches not only to see if they have the experience and education to help you make it all happen, but to see if they vibe with you. While getting recommendations is always a good idea, keep in mind that your best friend's or mentor's coach may not be the coach for you.

In her *Inc.* magazine article, "10 Questions for Picking Your Perfect Life Coach," life coach Jessica Zemple recommends asking yourself a few questions before interviewing prospective coaches. Ask yourself what kind of coach you need (business, holistic, etc.), how much you are willing to spend, and what kind of approach you need to make things happen.[3] Once you have those questions answered, it's time to start researching coaches.

While there are many generalists, you will likely want to make sure your coach has the proper applicable experience and training (more than a weekend boot camp) in the area you are looking to improve. For instance, if you are looking to start a business, a business coach or life coach with entrepreneurial experience and education will benefit you most. If you are looking to improve your health, you may look to a life coach with training in wellness fields such as nutrition, exercise, stress reduction, or spirituality.

After finding candidates in the field you are looking to improve, make sure you can afford to consistently work with them for the period of time you need to realize your intention or goals. If someone costs too much, you may need to wait to work with that person or work with someone else that fits your current budget. Finally, find someone that "gets" you. You need to be open and honest with your life coach, so if you don't find someone you feel comfortable with, it's going to be an uphill battle. This is your time, money, and happiness— respect it and choose well.

YOUR PERSONAL LIFE COACH: ADVICE FROM MARIE

I know by now you have to be feeling the positive life coach vibes. To keep the momentum going while you are starting your own life coach search, I asked Marie to give three general pieces of advice most women need to hear. Try one or more for progress you can build on.

#1: Mindset Is Everything: Embrace "Figureoutable"

Marie's mother liked to use the word "figureoutable," and that apple didn't fall far from the tree. Figureoutable is really a mindset, a belief that there is a solution to any problem; you just need to find it. Sometimes finding it is easy, other times it will take mass amounts of creativity, but if you believe it and put action behind the belief, you'll figure it out. If we get stuck in analysis paralysis, all thinking and no doing, we don't make it to the solution.

> "Clarity comes from engagement, not thought, so you need to be consistently focusing on taking action."

Marie talks about the importance of action by saying, "If you want to experience some progress, we just need to take an action. Clarity comes from engagement, not thought, so you need to be consistently focusing on taking action. Action is the antidote to fear. Action is the only way that we're going to turn that dream into reality." Action will help you figure it out!

#2: Stop Stressing

The advice Marie would give her younger self is the same advice she is giving you—stop stressing! "Give yourself a little more space and grace to enjoy the journey. I was such a worrier. I was so nervous and anxious in my twenties believing that life was passing me by too fast and I wasn't where I was supposed to be. I think that is a chronic condition that can follow us around through life, where we have this ongoing narrative that we should be further along than we are. All it does is rob us of the joy, exhilaration, and appreciation of each moment as we live it. We have to be grateful for it," Marie says.

> "I think that we have to ask ourselves at every stage and season of life, what is going to help us thrive?"

No new news here: Women are especially impacted by stress. According to the American Psychological Association, "Only 52 percent of men say it is very/extremely important to manage stress, compared to 68 percent of women. And 63 percent of men say they're doing enough to manage their stress, compared to 51 percent of women."[4] Long-term stress robs us of our health,[5] productivity, and happiness, so find a way to manage it.

#3: Replace Work-Life Balance with a Seasonal Approach

It's one of the ultimate catchphrases, "work-life balance," but is it really possible? According to Marie, no. "I think it's fiction. I think that we have to ask ourselves at every stage and season of life, what is going to help us thrive? When I was working on writing my book *Everything Is Figureoutable*, my life felt terribly out of balance, but I was really happy and healthy," she says. She goes on to liken balance to a state of static: "When you think about balancing on something, you almost have to hold your breath and have everything not move, because otherwise you're going to fall off and you're not going to be in balance anymore. I think life is too fluid for that."

> "I think that you do have to create some routines and rituals for yourself."

Instead of looking for the mythical unicorn of work-life balance, recognize where you are right now. Are you burning the candle at both ends? Maybe you have to, but only for a few weeks because that's what life requires at that moment. Once you're done, enjoy a period of rest, and ease into a less demanding schedule to reboot.

Even if you are in a place of go-go-go, there are ways to weave self-care into your days. Marie advises, "I think that you do have to create some routines and rituals for yourself. I know for me, I'm moving my body every day. It doesn't always have to be an hour. For the past few weeks, I've been doing these free yoga classes online, some of which are 15 to 20 minutes. When I'm done, I feel fantastic." Carve out a little time for yourself, no matter how short, to give yourself a moment of bliss every day.

• • •

So let's reflect: You know what a life coach is as compared with a therapist or mentor. Everyone can use one (Oprah and Bill Gates are loud and proud about theirs, so there must be something to it). You've now learned how to prepare yourself for coaching, how to vet a coach, and what needs to happen to be successful. You've even received a few key pieces of advice to get you started while you find your own. What are you waiting for? Make it happen!

7

BET ON YOURSELF

Defining Your Meaning by Impact

Success is not measured in the amount of dollars you make,
but the amount of lives you impact.
—UNKNOWN

In this chapter, we're going to focus on the intentional act of working for a purpose, not just a paycheck. The work you do should compensate you in a way that is fulfilling, help you stay true to yourself and what matters to you, boost your confidence, deepen connections with others, and bring you joy. Ideally, it should also make a positive impact, by making a way for others, improving lives, or inspiring others to pursue their intentions as well.

MILLENNIALS AND THE PURPOSE-DRIVEN CAREER

Studies show millennials are constantly seeking purpose in what they do for a living, but at the same time want to know how their job is helping them get to the top. In a Gallup poll, researchers found that millennials looked for a few key attributes when choosing a job: working with a purpose, having opportunities for development, having ways to increase their strengths rather than focusing on their weakness, being able to have conversations with supervisors, and having coaches rather than bosses.[1] They're constantly questioning where they are going next and why, and interestingly enough, how their rise will benefit others in addition to themselves. Consider this: What do you want your life's work to be? Will it affect others, and if so, how?

My challenge to you is to ask yourself, "If I didn't do the work that I do, whose life would be worse off?" It is in answering questions like this where you will find meaning and impact, or the need for it. Need an example to get started? Look at late Supreme Court justice Ruth Bader Ginsberg. When we think of women who paved the way for other women (and let's face it, pretty much everyone), the so-named "Notorious RBG" is an incomparable figure. She not only fought to be a lawyer and judge (both rarities at the time for women); she also made major legal contributions for women, making it possible for women to have checking accounts and loans without a male cosigner, preserving women's right to choose an abortion, protecting pregnant women in the workplace, making strides toward bridging the pay gap between men and women, and being the "key vote" in granting the right to same-sex marriages.[2] Consider the butterfly effect—how many women were able to pursue their purpose because of her actions and inspiration? Without Justice Ginsberg, where would women be today?

Now it's easy to think about purpose in relation to job title, especially in the instance of Justice Ginsberg, but does a job title really mean anything? I believe it's more important to define your career by the impact you want to have than by the title you want to hold. Titles have their function; after all, they do indicate a sort of "workplace status" and give a subtle (if not always correct) indicator of the respect with which one needs to address another. They assign a hierarchy in the workplace and an indication of who holds power in the organization. However, fancy titles can sometimes be more harmful than helpful, and in some cases, they can be downright toxic to the work culture. Some companies will give title promotions to retain employees when the company doesn't have other compensation to give. In his article "The Dark Side of Job Title Inflation," Kurt Wilkin, entrepreneur and cofounder of recruiting firm and strategic talent consultancy HireBetter, states that this can create a major problem for the company, as people's titles can evolve past their actual skill set when the company grows. The company then has to either move these people around or let them go.[3] The individuals suffer because they head into a job market where their title, say, CFO, is more akin to a glorified office manager than a C-suite executive. Something like this can happen if you chase titles instead of purpose. It's the difference between saying, "I'm a Supreme Court justice," and having the intention of being a Supreme Court justice who will make the world a better, more inclusive, fairer place for everyone.

When Arlan Hamilton decided to become a venture capitalist, she didn't just do it with the title "venture capitalist" in mind. She did it with the intention of investing in startup founders who were often overlooked and underestimated by the white male venture capitalists that dominate the industry.

MEET ARLAN HAMILTON

Arlan Hamilton's approach to intention has far-reaching impact. She went from managing arena-level tours for musicians like popstar Jason Derulo to launching a venture capital fund, Backstage Capital, for startup founders like herself who are women, people of color, or LGBTQ+ entrepreneurs.

Arlan didn't have a Wall Street background or even a college degree, and found herself homeless during the time period she was pitching Backstage Capital to investors. Deeply rooted in her conviction she could raise the money and her intention to help underrepresented entrepreneurs, Arlan has gone on to invest millions of dollars in nearly 200 startups, including Trim-It, an app-powered mobile barbershop; Unchartered Power, a company that transforms anything that moves into renewable energy; and Hostfully, a platform that helps vacation rental companies manage and scale their businesses.

Growing up near Dallas, Texas, Arlan was entrepreneurial by the third grade. In a story Arlan recounted to CNBC, her mother would buy bulk candy at places like Costco and Sam's Club, and then Arlan would turn around and sell each piece at a profit.[4] At 15, she took a job as a cashier at a pizza place and rose to become an assistant manager by the time she graduated high school.

Though she performed well in high school, even graduating with honors, she hated it, because she couldn't ask questions or discover more beyond what textbooks provided. That sense of insatiable curiosity would follow her through her life and help her bring her intention to fruition.

Arlan decided to skip college. When she was 21, she wanted to see one of her favorite bands go on tour, so she reached out to the Norwegian punk-pop group to see if she could arrange the tour for the band. She had no experience, but the band agreed, and soon she was learning on the job.

"I didn't know what that meant at the time. I didn't know how to do that. I taught myself how to book a tour before there was Google and Twitter and all of that to make it happen. I booked the two-month-long tour in the summer. The band came out. I spent the whole time on the road with the band and fell in love with the whole vibe of it, even though no money was involved. We were just playing for dinner. It was just so much fun," she recalls.

Arlan decided to turn that fun into a career. She reached out to a hundred tour and production managers to network, receiving twenty responses, three in-person meetings, and one meeting that eventually turned into a job with singer-songwriter CeeLo Green. She would later go on to manage arena-level touring for Jason Derulo and Toni Braxton. However, as much as she enjoyed the work, event management wasn't fulfilling for Arlan.

She noticed that lots of celebrities were investing in startups. Curious, she researched and found that women, Black and brown, and

LGBTQ+ startup founders were overlooked and undervalued. She dug deeper and talked to founder upon founder, who couldn't even "get into the room" to make a pitch to try to get funding. That inspired her to build a business that would help these underrepresented founders scale their businesses.

The amount of money going to women founders is growing, but continues to lag behind investments in startups run by men. "In the U.S., startups with at least one female founder made up 23.8 percent of all venture capital investments in 2019," according to a report from financial data and software firm PitchBook. "In 2010, that figure was just 12.6 percent."[5]

According to a 2020 report from the US Securities and Exchange Commission, just 1 percent of venture capital–backed startups were led by Black founders between 2013 and 2017. Latino and Middle Eastern founders fared only slightly better at 2 percent. Asian founders led 18 percent of VC-backed startups, while the remaining 77 percent were led by white founders during that period.[6]

Eventually Arlan found her way to a two-week program for investors in training at Stanford University, partially funded by a scholarship. While in the Bay Area, she set up meetings with investors and founders. After about three years of knocking on doors and writing a blog telling people about the opportunity to fund businesses founded by underrepresented groups, she got a first yes in the form of a $25,000 check. Soon Backstage Capital was born.

As managing partner of Backstage, Arlan leads a team that identifies investments for the fund. She remains active finding new companies to invest in and finds there is no shortage of women, people of color, and people in the LGBTQ+ community that have concepts or companies to invest in. When we spoke, Arlan told me about a pitch event for women founders that she had just attended.

"You just see the creativity and just the execution of what they worked on—and none of them had raised capital outside of their bank accounts," she says. "How are they being overlooked? The ones that caught my eye the most—they were so expert in their field. They were just so right for what they were working on."

THE EXPONENTIAL EFFECTS OF IMPACT

Arlan created a microcosm of diversity with Backstage Capital, not only in investing in underrepresented founders, but in empowering others to take a seat at the table. Rather than decide whom to invest in strictly on her own, she empowers her team to go out and find diverse investments to present to her.

"I love that. Everyone on the team, it's a small team right now, has a different criterion, and they are bringing different companies and ideas," she says. In essence, she's invited the people in her internal organization to bring their own intention to work and helps build out those chain reactions of change as well.

In addition to funding people underrepresented in the startup space, and encouraging the members of her team to bring their own intentions to the table, Arlan is also focused on making sure the historical table-sitters see the manifestation of her intention. An experience she had at an effort launched by the University of Oxford's Saïd Business School to build ventures that benefit society and develop ethical leaders illustrates how important her mere presence might be.

She explains: "I'm an advisor at Oxford Foundry, and I also fund, with my mother, one of its first scholarships for a Black scholar. So I was talking to these two students who were both white men working on things. And I think that's just as important to me, for me to be representing someone they need to pitch to so they can get used to that." Everyone, on both sides of the table, needs to embrace the new normal.

Earvin "Magic" Johnson, not only one of the greatest basketball players of all time but a successful investor with intention, said something at Upfront Summit in Los Angeles in 2016 that hits on this point. "You have to look like America looks because right now the tech sector doesn't look like America," he said during a panel discussion. Arlan is encouraging others and doing her best to change that for all the sectors that lack diversity.

> "Take as much time as you can with research and in guiding the blueprint and strategy of what you want to do; then reflect on what you have done and what you can do better."

FOUR MAJOR INSIGHTS: ADVICE FROM ARLAN

After talking to Arlan, I took away four major insights I thought would be invaluable to millennial women. These pieces of advice can help you really dive deep into your intention and excavate the true impact you can have on the world around you. If you haven't yet figured out your big picture, this section will be especially valuable to you.

#1: The Importance of Research and Experimentation

We've already discussed a few ways to formulate an intention, and Arlan had some great advice on this particular topic: "Take as much time as you can with research and in guiding the blueprint and strategy of what you want to do; then reflect on what you have done and what you can do better. It does not mean to spend the rest of your life just thinking about something and not executing on it." She believes preparation will save you time, money, and heartache, never forgetting that time itself is also money. Experimentation is wonderful and should be done, but always prepare as much as you can in advance. Do the research.

Don't know where to start? There is no shortage of quizzes out there that claim to point you toward your life's purpose. However, in all the discussions I've had and the research I've done, it generally comes down to three questions:

- What drives me?
- What energizes me?
- What am I willing to sacrifice for?

Most times, you will have to fund your own intention, at least in the beginning, so it needs to be something you are committed to and enjoy working toward, even without immediate monetary reward. Once you figure that out, like Arlan says, research and experiment. You have to do, not just think.

#2: Be Prepared

Being prepared is another skill you need to bring your intention to life. You won't be able to foresee everything, but controlling the controllable is a surefire way to succeed. Arlan remembers how important being prepared was when she received her first check to start investing: "When I got the first check to invest in someone, I had already done the research on who I was going to invest in, and boom, I started that day. I didn't have to waste any time or lose any time. You're never going to be able to figure it all out ahead of time, I won't lie to you, but you have much more control over where your foot falls next."

#3: Understand Your Unique Value

Sometimes the most impactful part of your intention is that you are the one bringing it forth. "I wanted to be bold and reflect something else. So it was kind of easy to look at venture capital and see that there are only a few Black women and that shouldn't be the case. I want to put the spotlight on 'us' as a person. It took me until I was 36 to understand that."

Let's take a second to check in: Where are you in your intention? Why is it bespoke to fit you? How will you leverage your uniqueness to bring it to fruition?

#4: Eschew Impostor Syndrome

While not exclusive to women, impostor syndrome is an infectious parasite that clings to women in business, especially women of color. Impostor syndrome, defined as "the idea that you've only succeeded due to luck, and not because of your talent or qualifications," is an especially nefarious undercurrent that shakes women and people of color in the workplace as well as in society at large. While men do experience it, women are uniquely affected by it, according to Pauline Rose Clance and Suzanne Imes, the psychologists that coined the term.[7] Why? Simply put, when we don't see many people who look like us succeeding in our respective fields, we are less likely to believe ourselves capable of it. According to Lean In's 2019 research, for every 100 men that are brought onto teams and elevated to management, only 72 women experience the same thing. Women hold 38 percent of managerial positions, whereas men hold 62 percent.[8] Additionally, Catalyst reports that less than 5 percent of board seats are held by women of color.[9]

Rather than give in to the feelings of unworthiness, focus again on what makes you worthy of being there and why you must be there. Arlan says to remember, "Your expertise is probably more so than you think. In general, we are all equal. Why should someone, just because of the color of their skin, or their gender, or their family line, or how much money they have in the bank—why should someone else get a piece of what's yours? That makes no sense to me anymore. I'm done with that."

• • •

Are you inspired by Arlan? My hope is that this chapter has given you a light into the importance of having an intention that makes an impact and you are armed with some tools to get started. If you're still searching out the full depth of your intention, keep doing the work. You'll get there soon enough!

8

WHAT TO DO WHEN WORK ISN'T WORKING

Finding Balance Leads to Success

Success is the quality of our lives,
not just the quantity of our achievements.
—ADAM GRANT

Sometimes you start your career with what feels like a clear intention. Hard work? Check. Great education? Double check. Impressive companies on your résumé. Triple check!

And even with all that, the unexpected can happen. Actually for most people, the unexpected *will* happen. Life is sure to throw you a number of curveballs along the way, whether it's health troubles, family crises, or changes in your profession. Or maybe one day you get real with yourself, and you acknowledge that you're just not feeling the path you chose. For some people, the curveballs make starting a business an attractive idea.

The rate of new entrepreneurs starting businesses rose sharply from 2019 to 2020, according to the Kauffman Foundation, which studies entrepreneurship. Some of that increase was likely due to the disruption related to the coronavirus pandemic. However, the number of new startups had already been growing over the previous few years, according to Kauffman.[1]

Women, in particular, have embraced the startup life in greater numbers. Men still outpace women when it comes to starting new businesses, but women in the United States are catching up for the first time in years, according to the Global Entrepreneurship Monitor's 2019 survey, with women starting ventures at 91 percent the pace of men.[2]

Starting a business from scratch comes with a lot of risk and no regular paycheck (at least at first) and can dominate your life. Entrepreneurs often bemoan not taking vacations or getting to spend time with friends. So why take the leap? Women are looking for more flexibility to accommodate family needs, to have more control over their future, and to follow their passions, Caroline Castrillon, a career and life coach, explains in a 2019 *Forbes* article. Other factors include wanting to advance more quickly, charge what they are worth, and get off the corporate roller coaster of layoffs, restructurings, and buyouts.[3]

Changing careers isn't new. In the period from 2015 to 2016, 6.2 million Americans changed careers, according to government data.[4] Intrigued? Well, here's some really great news for women craving a change: The advances in technology and the development of social media have cut through some of the traditional barriers to entrepreneurship. Online resources, software, and apps make it possible for people to successfully operate a business from their sofas using laptops, or from their cars on smartphones. Startup costs are remarkably lower than they once were, allowing more people to take control of their destiny by calling their own shots through entrepreneurship. This opportunity is especially palpable among millennials, who have grown up with technology in a way that sets them apart from previous generations.

"You can become an influencer on Instagram and make money. You can make money off YouTube videos; you can start your own tech company. Now, some of these things, a lot of these things, fail, but it's a whole different set of career possibilities that weren't open to previous generations because we didn't have the technology to allow us to do all of these things," says Stephanie Creary, assistant professor of management at the University of Pennsylvania's Wharton School. "The lever or driver around career decisions for millennials in particular is the fact that there is technology out there that influences how they view themselves and how others view them."

In my chat with Creary, she spoke about the ways that millennial women (and many millennial men) move through their lives and careers differently than did previous generations when it comes to expectations and desires around having families. "This generation has really pushed the envelope on setting their own expectations for themselves and trying to find a work situation that allows them to do and become that person who they want to become," Creary told me.

Sometimes becoming the person you want to become means setting a new intention as your life evolves. That intention could be something that fuels your passion. It might solve a need that you identify. It may benefit from some of those previous intentions (and goals) you set for yourself earlier in your education and career—as it did with business partners Georgene Huang and Romy Newman.

MEET GEORGENE HUANG

Before Georgene Huang, the CEO and cofounder of career site Fairygodboss, started the company, she was among the New York (and global) financial elite. She was head of institutional product at financial information and media company Dow Jones & Co., which owns the *Wall Street Journal* and *Barron's*, two publications that are required reading for anyone who wants to know what's going on in markets and in business; and she was previously managing director at Bloomberg Ventures, now known as Bloomberg Beta, an incubator for startups. Bloomberg, as you may know, is a financial media and data company whose Bloomberg terminal is considered among the most powerful tools to research, analyze, and keep up with information covering an immense range of markets and businesses. Along the way, she also worked at Lehman Brothers, which was among the biggest US investment banks before it filed for bankruptcy as part of the 2008 global financial crisis.

Georgene's life began thousands of miles from that world. Her family immigrated to the United States from Taiwan and settled in the San Francisco Bay Area. Her father, a blue-collar worker, was what she describes as a "tiger dad" who nurtured her desire to achieve. "He told me 'You don't get an A. You get an A-plus. Forget about Bs.'" To him, anything less just wasn't acceptable.

As she grew up, Georgene watched her mother navigate her own education and career in technology, and it made an impression on her. Her mother was one of very few women in the field at that time. Observing her mother's experience left an impression on her that being different shouldn't be a deterrent to pursuing what she wanted.

Georgene didn't head toward Wall Street right away. Her early interests spanned music and law, and she pursued both with vigor. She initially studied the flute at a conservatory in San Francisco, but then transferred to Cornell University where she earned a degree in economics. Next, with her drive to excel, she headed back to the Bay Area to get a law degree from Stanford University with a goal of working in the judicial system. She passed the bar exam and landed at a prestigious law firm in New York. It didn't take long for her to realize she wasn't happy.

"I expected to put in long hours, but, I thought, this is just not as interesting as I think it should be. And I also am not making as much money as I should make if I'm going to work until midnight every Friday, because I had all these investment banker friends who were working just as hard as me and they were making more money than me," she recalls.

Georgene landed a position at investment bank Lehman Brothers and then transitioned to work in the private equity and hedge fund industries. But it may have been her role at Bloomberg Ventures that ignited the intention that grew a few years later. At Bloomberg Ventures, Georgene worked on building businesses from scratch. She was writing business plans, building the initial products, testing the products, and taking those ideas to market. It was thrilling. "That's where I got really excited. I felt better about doing those things than I did about the law, finance, or music," she says. Georgene followed her boss from Bloomberg to Dow Jones. At this point she and her future business partner Romy Newman, who also worked at Dow Jones, knew each other peripherally. "I would hear Georgene's voice on conference calls," Romy recalls.

Remember in the beginning of this chapter when I mentioned curveballs? Well, Georgene would soon encounter one of her own. Two years after she joined Dow Jones, she was laid off in a restructuring. She was also pregnant.

MEET ROMY NEWMAN

Stick with me and you'll find out how Georgene took that curveball thrown her way and created a new intention. But before we get there, you need to get to know Romy, who became a big part of bringing what became a shared intention with Georgene to life.

Romy Newman is the president and the cofounder of Fairygodboss. Born and raised in New York City, Romy spent a lot of time helping to raise her younger brother. Her parents were divorced, and both worked outside the home. Her mother had a big influence on her and her work ethic.

Romy thinks back: "I grew up with a mother who had a really big, ambitious career, and she worked really hard. She was a salesperson who earned only commission. So from a very young age, I knew what it was to make a sale. There was this very clear connection between the work she did and the money she received." Her mother also showed her the level of energy that was required to succeed, and it's something Romy used as she progressed in her career. Observing her mother also instilled an intention in her to always make sure she was secure financially.

"I have been very connected to earning money and making sure that I could provide for myself from a young age," Romy explains.

Romy's educational choices demonstrate that she wasn't messing around. Like Georgene, she chose prestigious schools that would give her a top-notch education and help her build an impressive set of credentials. She earned her bachelor's degree from Yale University and later got a master's in business administration from the Kellogg School of Management at Northwestern University.

Among her career stops, Romy worked at cosmetics giant Estée Lauder where she had started as an intern, and later she spent a few years working for a media consultancy. Next she moved onto what many people may have viewed as one her most enviable jobs.

"I got an opportunity to go work at Google, and I thought, wow, they're the best of the best," Romy recalls thinking. "This is going to be so exciting. It's so vibrant. I can't believe I get to go work at Google."

Landing a job with search and internet advertising behemoth Google Inc. (now Google LLC) is considered highly desirable among workers. A 2020 survey by Hired, a company that helps match tech workers with jobs in the industry, found that tech workers in the San Francisco Bay Area ranked Google as the top employer there (tied with Netflix). Google placed higher than many other tech companies, including Slack, LinkedIn, and Apple.[5]

Unlike the tech workers who want to work for Google—or love working there—Romy realized quickly that, for her, taking the job was a mistake.

"On the first day I was like, 'Oh my goodness, this isn't right for me.' I was only there seven months, and I could just see the whole time I was there, it was not a fit," she says.

Romy landed next at Dow Jones & Co. where she worked for the *Wall Street Journal,* first in a finance and strategy role. She moved up the ladder in sales leadership, overseeing the launch of major products, and finally was promoted to oversee revenue for the *Journal's* digital product suite. Despite her success there, Romy was ready for a change. The corporate environment was constraining her.

"Throughout my career, the review feedback I always got was like, 'Romy, stop trying to do everybody else's job; stay in your lane.' And then when Georgene and I started working together, it was like I didn't have to stay in my lane," she says.

MEET FAIRYGODBOSS

Though Romy and Georgene had been coworkers and knew each other, they didn't know each other well. When we left Georgene's story, she had been laid off from Dow Jones and was pregnant. This is where their stories merge.

Georgene was in the midst of a job search and wanted information on how women were treated at various companies and what their maternity leave benefits were. The problem? This information wasn't online, or seemingly anywhere. Rather than bemoan this lack of information, her experience at Bloomberg Ventures gave her the know-how to see that there was a real "white space" that needed a product to fill it. So instead of looking for a job, she started looking for a cofounder to start her new business to fulfill her new intention. She wanted to create a space that would help women advance their careers with information, resources, and community to meet their specific needs.

Georgene was put in touch with Romy through a mutual friend, and Fairygodboss was born.

Fairygodboss is the largest career community for women and a place where millions of women are finding their next job. Through its community, job board, employee reviews, curated content, and hiring events, it works to help women achieve their career goals. It democratizes access to career advice, mentorship, and networking and improves the workplace through greater transparency, while also helping major companies like Apple, Johnson & Johnson, Home Depot, and Deloitte attract, engage, and hire women, especially in hard-to-fill technology roles.

Fairygodboss tailors to the questions and needs of women. Women come to look for jobs with quality companies. Women can find other women to network with and ask for advice. There are also webinars women can attend, like "Real Talk and Tips for a Career in STEM," "Landing Your First People Leader Role," and "How to Take Ownership of Your Career." In short, it's a free platform for women to advance their careers.

"Whether you're actively looking for a job or you're just looking for help with a work problem or issue, that's what we are for the user base we have. And that is how we fulfill our social mission, which is about helping women achieve their career goals," says Georgene. She goes on to say, "I think we help tell the story and highlight the role models that are not always front and center so that women can look at an employer through a new lens."

According to Georgene and Romy, Fairygodboss creates a bridge of understanding between women in the workplace and the concerns and needs of their partner companies. Organizations can read what their current and former employees are saying, which allows companies to solve problems they may or may not know were impacting the experience of women in their ranks. Not only does that help companies attract highly qualified female candidates from outside their organizations, but companies also can recruit from and attract their employee base from within Fairygodboss. It's a win-win for all sides.

Georgene and Romy both had impressive résumés before they joined forces to launch Fairygodboss. The lessons and skills that they accumulated along the way gave them key tools and perspective they would later use when starting their own business.

That foundation supported a new intention. Georgene and Romy had a problem that they were attempting to solve for themselves.

They found that they weren't alone in their pursuit to find flexibility and fulfillment in their careers. Technology—through launching the Fairygodboss site—served as the key to help women with their job search by helping them assess workplace flexibility and connect with likeminded women to solve career challenges. Their intentionality brought them together as business partners and allowed them to focus on an issue that was important to each of them. They saw a need and took action, and that action resulted in a thriving business.

GEORGENE AND ROMY'S TIPS TO HELP YOU PIVOT

Even if entrepreneurship isn't your path and technology isn't your thing, Georgene and Romy have some great advice to help you pivot as your intention evolves.

#1: Don't Limit Yourself

After being limited by society for so long, it's no wonder a majority of women still limit themselves. There's a lot of inside chatter about "I can't do this" or "Who am I to think I can do X?" The double-edged sword is that many women who do accomplish their goals feel some variation of impostor syndrome.

"I would say be very careful not to limit yourself based on your own definitions of what you can or can't do. Founding Fairygodboss has taught me that in so many ways," Romy says.

When Georgene told her they needed to start writing articles, Romy, initially, wasn't sure if she measured up in that category. Having come from the *Wall Street Journal*, where journalists were the best of the best, in her view she wasn't qualified to write. Georgene, however, empowered her to do it and made her feel like she had the right to write an article.

"Don't let yourself box yourself in. Don't limit what you can do. Don't feel like you need permission to do anything. You can do anything you set your heart to, and there's no downside. Just try. The only way you get better is just by trying, and don't be afraid of doing new things."

Still a little gun-shy? Georgene understands and suggests supporting yourself by doing your research and gathering information, as she did when she decided to break into finance by taking the job at Lehman Brothers.

"You can read all the books in the world, and you can do the informational interviews. I did all of that. I read them. I started reading everything Warren Buffett had ever said. I read every finance book I could get my hands on," Georgene recalls.

Don't just stop there. Remember, you can also take a multimedia approach and read blogs, listen to podcasts, or watch TED Talks.

#2: Find Community/Network/Mentors

As I've said in past chapters, you are not alone. Find your community, your squad, your network, your mentor, or whatever you may call it and learn from that resource. If you still can't find what you are looking for, Romy is sure you can find a career-related community at Fairygodboss.

Romy explains: "We have a few different ways that women can engage with our site. There are communities everywhere online, right? But until us, there has not been a definitive destination where women come together to share the challenges and experiences of a career. We've talked to users, and women have a lot of uncertainty. We have this community feed where women are coming together to ask questions. But more importantly, the number one reason women use our platform is that they want to help other women. That's what our name is about. We want to be the place where women help other women and support them."

#3: Keep Your Personal Brand Front of Mind

We now live in a personal brand world. What you do, how you present yourself, and how you are perceived are all elements of your personal brand.

Ask yourself, "What is your unique selling proposition?," Romy says. After you decide what that is, articulate it with examples and practice it. Keep in mind you will not be in the room when someone is deciding whether or not you'll get promoted. So somebody better know what you're good at when you're not there.

Women struggle with a career-limiting myth that Romy wants them to discard. "You cannot just think if you put your head down and do your best work, you'll get promoted. Unfortunately, that's not true," Romy says. Employers need to know you, and to make sure they do, you need to refine, project, and back up your personal brand.

#4: Know Your Value (and Don't Be Afraid to Talk About It)

Ask a woman what she needs to work on, and you'll get a list a mile long of this and that, personal and professional. Ask her to list what she excels at, and you may get a few mumbled answers. Of course, this isn't universal, but it is often true.

"At our events, we actually force participants to go around and brag about themselves. I see women, enormously successful women, panic in the face of having to say something about themselves, about what they're great at," Romy says.

Women, historically, have been socially conditioned to be modest and not brag or even acknowledge their accomplishments (though thankfully we are seeing that culture shift). When women don't talk about their accomplishments, it can take longer for them to experience the rewards of their hard work. Not satisfied with a potentially long wait? Good, neither are we! Romy's number one piece for women is, "Think about yourself as your publicist." You are the client and need the right publicity. So go ahead and brag!

9

TRIUMPH OVER TRIALS

Relentless Determination to Succeed

Every journey begins with the first step of articulating
the intention, and then becoming the intention.
—BRYANT MCGILL

M oney is one of the most stressful things in many millennial women's lives. Not having a handle on it can be damaging to women in the workplace. It is only when we are fully confident in our finances that we can be truly secure in our careers. We as women must be intentional, strategic, and attentive to our financial goals, because those behaviors result in higher performance, compensation, and wealth. In this chapter, we are going to get down to the dollars and cents of the matter.

WEALTH AND THE MILLENNIAL WOMAN

When you think of wealth, what do you think of? Is it a portfolio bursting with investments in socially responsible companies, or are you thinking of a Birkin and a Benz? Based on Instagram, it would be easy to assume that millennials are focused on spending lavishly on a lifestyle that they can't afford. However, there are millennials who are saving for their financial future and are focused on the bigger picture.

The Federal Reserve reports that millennials have a smaller median net worth—about 9 percent lower—than that of their Gen X counterparts when they were the same age.[1] This may seem worrisome, but millennials' investment in their education will likely lead to higher earnings and increase their net worth. But if women have to wait to make more money in their future, what does that mean for investing and building wealth in their twenties and early thirties?

Up to 34 percent of women aged 18–29 have nothing in their retirement savings, according to a March 2020 survey conducted by CNBC and investing app Acorns in partnership with SurveyMonkey.[2] Among millennial women living with male partners, 54 percent left long-term financial planning to their partner, according to another 2020 study by investment bank UBS that surveyed women with at least $250,000 in investable assets.[3]

What's got women so spooked about investing? A report by Merrill Lynch and research consultancy Age Wave suggests that lack of knowledge (60 percent) and lack of confidence (34 percent) are to blame.[4]

Later in this chapter, we'll talk about how even with a little money and time, many women (and men!) can start to build a more secure financial future. But before we do, I want to discuss one more element that puts additional pressure on women and people of color.

THE REALITY OF WEALTH INEQUALITY

Wealth inequality, also called economic inequality, refers to gaps in "income or wealth between richer and poorer households."[5] According to the Pew Research Center, the rise in economic inequality in the United States is due to a number of factors such as technological change, the decline of unions, the devaluation of the minimum wage, and globalization. When economic inequality rises, those who are less affluent aren't as likely to find opportunities for upward mobility, which then just perpetuates the already broken system.

Let's now factor in two other things that also affect wealth inequality: gender and race. In a report released in 2020 on global inequality,

Oxfam, an international charitable organization focused on eradicating poverty, stated that "wealth inequality is in part because of gender inequality."[6]

I am not one to be overly didactic and try not to be, even in this book; however, I will say this: Do not believe the fake news out there that says there is not a wealth gap.

A September 2020 report from the US Federal Reserve showed that, in its words, "long-standing and substantial wealth disparities between families in different racial and ethnic groups were little changed since the last survey in 2016." The Fed's analysis compared data from 2016 and 2019, and it showed that the typical white family has eight times the wealth of the typical Black family and five times the wealth of the typical Hispanic family."[7] The report goes on to say that Black families have less than 15 percent of the wealth of white families. Hispanic families have a slightly higher percentage, and a group defined only as "other," which includes those identifying as Asian, American Indian, Alaska Native, Native Hawaiian, Pacific Islander, or other races, is somewhat higher than its Hispanic counterpart. The numbers are there, in symbolic black and white, that wealth inequality is a very real thing in the United States.

"Economic inequality is a major issue in this country, and it has led to a great deal of social unrest. Yes, it was caused by police brutality. There's no question about it. However, civil unrest is also the result of unfairness that exists in our society," says Mellody Hobson, chairman of the board of trustees of Ariel Investment Trust and co-CEO and president of Chicago-based and minority-owned Ariel Investments LLC, which, as of June 30, 2021, managed more than $16 billion in assets for investors.

If it feels like I've painted a bleak picture of where women and minorities stand financially, that's not my aim. What I want is for you to understand the challenges women like you may face and to underscore how important it is for you to get ahead of those challenges.

I know from experience that we can take charge of our money and secure a robust financial future. And when it comes to understanding how to clear those hurdles and vanquish the challenges, I knew there was no better person to sit down with than Mellody Hobson.

MEET MELLODY HOBSON

Ariel, where Mellody Hobson first began as an intern, helps a range of investors increase their wealth.

"I'm a capitalist. I believe in the capitalist system," says Mellody, whose impressive list of achievements includes becoming chairwoman of the board of Starbucks Corp. and serving on boards of companies such as JPMorgan Chase & Co., Estée Lauder Cos., and DreamWorks Animation. When Mellody became chairwoman of the board of Starbucks in March 2021, she was the only Black women in such a role in any company in the Standard & Poor's 500 index.

Mellody is one of the highest-profile African American corporate directors on the globe. She is so influential that a fictional character on television's *The Good Wife* was created in her likeness.

"I have not found any system anywhere in the world that works better than ours, but it has to work for everyone. It must be more fairly allocated. All people, no matter their race, gender, sexual orientation, or any other characteristic that defines them, should have the opportunity to succeed. It is important to understand that our decisions drive our future. They really do," Mellody says. Her passion for creating a secure financial future has extended to her highly visible work as a regular financial contributor for multiple media outlets over the last two decades, including ABC News. While her work on many topics has garnered national media attention, educating people about money hits closest to home. As part of its mission, Ariel works to "make savings and investing a seminal area of focus for the African American community." It's done that through a range of activities, including financial literacy training for children and families.

Mellody is the expert I thought of first when I put together my dream list of people to talk to about money for this book. Mellody has achieved the kind of career and life that many aspire to have. It would be easy to assume that she enjoyed a great deal of privilege. But that wasn't her reality growing up in Chicago. The youngest of six siblings in a single-parent household, she recalls a tough life, one where money was scarce, and the threats of going without electricity and gas and getting evicted were very real. That motivated her.

"I wanted to wake up knowing where I was going to sleep, knowing what I was going to eat, knowing that there was going to be lights and gas," she says.

Even though she was young, Mellody was very aware of the power of money, but in a way that most kids weren't. From the start, she wasn't like everyone else, a fact she herself knew. She explains, "I would say that from the very, very beginning, I was a really odd child, and extraordinarily focused and driven. I had a mother who supported it, even though my mom was very introverted and would not be an out-front personality on anything but on supporting me. She was just very present. She indulged all of my idiosyncrasies."

One of those idiosyncrasies was asking people to bring back newspapers from places they visited just so she could read the local news in another city. She stayed up until two in the morning doing homework and refused to believe her mother when the occasional snow day would close schools. To get her homework done, she retreated to the bathroom, using the closed toilet seat as a makeshift desk—sometimes running the water in the bathtub to drown out noise from elsewhere in the apartment.

Mellody took responsibility for herself very early in life. Her mother helped ingrain this independence in her. She remembers: "Anything we wanted to do, we had to figure out how to do it ourselves. So if I wanted to go to a birthday party, my mom would say, even when I was a kid, 'How are you getting there?'" She always had to think ahead and devise a plan, a skill that would be useful in Mellody's life, and certainly had a hand in her being the first person in her immediate family to graduate from college.

INTENTION: HAVE A PATH AND WALK IT

Mellody had a very clear intention from a young age: to have a better life. She speaks about her intention in such a way that you can hear the conviction that resonated within her then, and today. She says: "I was very, very focused on having a better life . . . full stop. You could not deter me from that. I was obsessed with school because I thought school was the way that I could have a better life. I was a child who was desperate to understand money—and I put the emphasis on the word 'understand' because if I understood it, I would know how to make it and keep it and have financial security. It's a direct line—my work is directly correlated to what was imprinted on me in terms of scarcity as a child."

Scarcity. I want you to pause here for a moment to think about that word and what it means. Mellody raises a key element in how we function when it comes to money—or any resource that is scarce in your life. We have the power to use scarcity to inspire us to learn, work harder, and achieve, as in Mellody's case. Or we can allow the fear of scarcity to rule us and, as a result, never take risks because we are afraid we will lose the little we have. As you read about how Mellody created her path, consider your relationship with scarcity.

Once you have an intention, how do you bring it to life? If you're Mellody, you chart a path. Mellody's intentions around her career played out in themes over decades.

In her twenties, she worked on proving she was the clutch player, proving to be indispensable. That meant working seven days a week, sometimes taking time on Saturday to take in a movie—usually alone so that she didn't have to coordinate schedules with anyone else. Her focus in that decade was to be at the disposal of Ariel founder John W. Rogers, Jr. She decided that "everything I do is around his schedule— around his time—to take work that he doesn't want to do away from him and to make myself indispensable," she recalls.

In her thirties, Mellody found that the foundation she laid in her twenties paid off. She had more than the financial security that she desired. At this point, she was laser-focused on excellence and trusted to be strategic and valued for generating ideas. Now in her fifties, Mellody has achieved an ownership position in Ariel and is focused on how she can impact the firm's legacy. "So this period of my life is less about financial security because I passed that test," Mellody says. "This period of my life is about what do I make of this influence and how do I create a lasting institution inside of Ariel?"

However, as we've already learned, even a great path can come to a fork, and you have to choose one road: the one you planned or another road with a new opportunity and potential risk. What do you do? In Mellody's case you make both work.

Mellody's decision came with a courtship, not from her husband, but from the very respected television broadcast journalist Diane Sawyer, who was anchoring *Good Morning America* at the time. Mellody recalls Diane calling her, saying, "I want you to think about doing *Good Morning America*." Mellody went on: "She said, 'We never, ever see people like you talking about money, and I think an entirely new group of people will listen to you.'" Diane Sawyer was essentially pitching her a job to be the show's money correspondent and change the face of money journalism in America. It was no small thing.

Like many of us, Mellody immediately focused on the hurdles. She loved her job. She was committed to Ariel. Undeterred, Diane suggested that she could work with her company to allow her to do both; she didn't have to choose one over the other. Mellody, having built a great deal of trust and value within Ariel ever since her twenties, was able to make it work and hasn't looked back since.

LOOKING FORWARD: ADVICE FROM MELLODY TO CREATE A STRONG FINANCIAL FUTURE

We've learned a lot from Mellody's example. Take the following advice from her, and you'll be on your way to building a strong financial future.

#1: Abandon the Rescue Fantasy

What is the rescue fantasy? Have you ever heard of the rescue fantasy? If not, have you ever seen a Disney princess cartoon pre-1990? A rescue fantasy is the (false) notion that someone is going to save you. Someone may be saving you from yourself, or from making a bad decision, or simply from making a decision, or from adulting in general. For most of history, women have been socially conditioned to believe that a man will rescue them from a wicked stepmother, an evil curse, a tower, or a car payment. This is dangerous for everyone, no matter one's gender identification. Mellody recalls a quote from singer Judy Collins, who left her financial matters to her manager for 20 years, only to find that she didn't have money to pay her taxes. She took the reins fast, saying, "As women, we were raised to have rescue fantasies, and I'm here to tell you, no one is coming."[8] This really resonated with Mellody. "I took full responsibility for myself. And I think that's a powerful, powerful thing to do," Mellody says.

> "As women, we were raised to have rescue fantasies, and I'm here to tell you, no one is coming."

Mellody has a great tip on how to do this—make a pledge. *Be warned:* This is not a step for the uncommitted! Serious people only need apply. Mellody advises: "Make a pledge, a date when you will not take money from your parents or any other family member anymore. Maybe the only thing you take from them is healthcare coverage until you're the age of 26. I really hope that the women who will be reading this may be working and therefore may have healthcare through their employer. I would say that the first step is to make that decision to be financially independent, and not to count on anyone." Want to be successful? Tell your family about your pledge; accountability breeds success.

#2: Have a Plan

Having a plan seems simple enough, right? Not really. Having a plan means really thinking about what you want to do, how you're going to execute it, and why you are the person who is best suited to do it. That way, when you are executing your plan, you'll be prepared. Think about how Mellody ordered her steps through her career. She went from being the indispensable player

> "Make that decision to be financially independent, and not to count on anyone."

at Ariel in her twenties to having an ownership stake today. None of that was by chance.

There are lots of ways to make a career plan. There are countless books and articles on the subject. Sites like Indeed and Forbes offer step-by-step plans to mapping out your career goals. If you feel like you can't DIY, lean on your support circle or hire a professional coach to help you put a plan down on paper.

#3: No Matter What You Do—Excel!

This next tip isn't revolutionary, but it's worth repeating time and time again: No matter what you do, do it 1,000 percent. It doesn't matter if you aren't doing your dream job now; do the job you're doing better than anyone else. Mellody echoes this sentiment: "I tell people if you told me tomorrow that I was going to be selling shoes at Neiman's in a year, I'd be the number one salesperson in the company. I do not look down on any job, and I'm confident that if given the opportunity to work hard, I can excel."

Where does that excellence come from? Well, intention of course. "I was very intentional about doing the work," Mellody explains. "I always did the work. I always put in the time, and I didn't complain about it. I just did it, however difficult it felt. It wasn't about the outcome. It was about the effort."

With that in mind, I want you to think about this: How can you excel at your current job today, tomorrow, next month, next year, and beyond? Write it down, and make it quantifiable. Make it real. Want to be more prepared for work? Show up 15 minutes early, or write out your to-do list before you leave work the day before, or even do both. These are actionable things that bring your intention to life.

#4: Start Investing: You Have to Play to Win

You may have read this advice and said, "With student loans, rent, the job market, etc., how can I afford to invest?" Well, you can't afford not to. Many people think that if they don't have $50,000 right now, they can't invest. Let Mellody disabuse you of this notion: "Take advantage of being able to invest—even a little money grows over the long term. It's not how much you invest at the end of the day. It's actually how long you let the money work for you. I call this my 'Time Is Money Speech' because it really is not only your personal time in terms of salary, but your time invested in the stock market that ultimately generates true financial independence and allows you to have the 'golden years' that people talk about when it comes to retiring. This concept is very hard to put your arms around when you're in your twenties or early thirties because you're not thinking about the fact that retirement is on the horizon. Sure, it's on the horizon far away, but the earlier you start, the better off you are."

Be sure to take advantage of any employer-match opportunities for your 401(k). If your employer offers a match, try your best to contribute enough to get the full amount your company will kick in. Micro-investing apps like Acorns, which work on a round-up theory of investing spare change, are a very low-cost barrier way to add other investments to your portfolio. You can also start with fairly low deposit amounts with Ellevest, a platform founded by a woman and designed with women in mind, or numerous other investment tools.

> "Take advantage of being able to invest—even a little money grows over the long term."

#5: Create a Wealth Sisterhood

Another tip we've heard before but bears mentioning again—create an accountability sisterhood, especially dealing with finances and building wealth. Mellody is especially passionate about this. "I love it because I think when you create a sisterhood around the financial conversation, that's really powerful. I think a sisterhood helps you hold each other accountable to it, even if it's the monthly contribution or what have you." For Mellody, it goes beyond just accountability; she believes there is even more value when you bring women together to support each other. She says: "I love the idea of women learning together. I think it's a very, very powerful forum for augmenting financial literacy and ultimately financial security. Women supporting women, fact or fiction in your view, but in my life, it's fact. I have had some of the most amazing women supporters ever, and I feel very strongly about being that person, even with peers."

. . .

After reading this chapter, learning Mellody's amazing story, and absorbing her advice, is your mind on your money and your money on your mind? I certainly hope so! Let's take a moment to reflect. Ask yourself a few questions:

- Can you take Mellody's pledge to take total control of your finances, if you haven't already taken the pledge?
- If not, what needs to happen for you to take that step?
- What are two things you can start doing this week to increase your wealth?
- What is stopping you from doing them? (Nothing? OK, let's get started then!)
- How much will you grow your wealth this year, next year, and five years from now?
- How will you do it?

Journal, do research, and set goals and figure out the steps you'll need to take to achieve them. Make a plan for your finances and career, and share it with your sisterhood.

I'm excited to see those wealth statistics start changing in the coming years!

10

AGENT OF CHANGE

Transforming Company Culture

Leadership is hard to define and good leadership even harder. But if you can get people to follow you to the ends of the earth, you are a great leader.

—INDRA NOOYI

We've talked about the detrimental effects a toxic workplace culture has on women. In this chapter, we're going to change gears to explore transforming culture, both professionally and personally, to create a more positive and inclusive space for us all to thrive in.

An agent of change is someone who promotes and enables transformation to happen within any group or organization. There's a lot of power in becoming an agent of change, and it can be applied in many ways. In this chapter you'll learn how to set an intention that will allow you to nurture your vision and become an agent of change yourself.

BE THE CHANGE YOU WISH TO SEE IN THE WORLD

It may feel like it is an understatement to say that there's a lot of change going on in the workplace (and beyond). Beyond the impact of the #MeToo movement, women are becoming more vocal about the wage gap, lack of female leadership, and company culture.

When I say "company culture," what do I mean? I think of it as an all-encompassing term that covers employee experiences, attitudes, opinions, leadership behaviors, and business models. Right now we are living in an exciting (sometimes exasperating) time where a successful workplace culture shifts the focus from diversity targets to inclusive environments—where people can be their authentic selves. So how do we change company culture? We become intentional. That means becoming the agents of the change that we'd like to see professionally and personally.

Let's talk about two change agents: filmmaker Ava DuVernay and attorney and technology nonprofit founder Reshma Saujani. As a director, producer, and writer, DuVernay is working to reshape Hollywood by embracing diversity, telling stories about Black people from behind the camera, and championing women and minority filmmakers. On the screen, she has done this through projects including the film *Selma*, based on the marches that led to the signing of the Voting Rights Act of 1965, and her Netflix limited series *When They See Us*, which tells the story of five Black and Latino young men who were wrongfully convicted of the brutal assault of a jogger in New York City's Central Park. She's stepped from behind the camera to introduce the Law Enforcement Accountability Project, a fund that helps activist storytellers in film, theater, photography, fine art, music, poetry, literature, sculpture, and dance tell true stories around police abuse of Black people.

Not only is DuVernay changing the narrative; she's changing the storytellers. She is amplifying Black voices, stories, and experiences to create not just art, but civil justice as well.

Reshma Saujani founded the nonprofit Girls Who Code, to close the gender gap in technology. Through a range of in-person education and online resources, the program encourages girls to build computer science skills that can lead to careers in video games, robotics, web design, engineering, and more. Girls Who Code has reached more than 300,000 girls worldwide.

In addition to her nonprofit, Saujani authored a book, *Brave, Not Perfect*, that clearly speaks to the pressures women feel to be perfect, describing it as a self-limiting prison sentence. She instead says we should be brave and take chances—it is the way we will dream bigger and find our own fulfillment.

DuVernay and Saujani are manifesting their intentions, uttering the very clear message: "If I can, you can too." Another amazing woman who is a major player, *pun intended*, when it comes to being an agent of change, is Michele Roberts.

MEET MICHELE ROBERTS

Michele Roberts is the former executive director of the National Basketball Players Association and is the first woman to head a major professional sports union in North America. Before she held this position, Michele was a celebrated attorney, once referred to by the *Washingtonian* as the "finest pure trial lawyer in Washington." She has worked as both a public defender and trial lawyer as well as an adjunct faculty member at Harvard Law School.

Michele was raised in a housing project in the South Bronx with her four siblings. Her parents split up when she was young, so being raised by a single mother had a major influence on her life. The family lived on public assistance, along with earnings from her mother's job as a maid in Midtown Manhattan, dinners that her mother would make and sell on weekends, and whatever other off-the-books jobs her mother could get. Michele went to public school until she earned a scholarship to a private school, the Masters School, in Dobbs Ferry, a section of the leafy Westchester County suburbs north of New York City.

Michele's mother would occasionally like to sit in courtrooms during trials in the Bronx, and eventually she brought her ever-inquisitive daughter with her. It wasn't long before Michele knew she wanted to be a lawyer.

"While I was watching those trials with my mom in the Bronx, you can imagine that most of the defendants looked just like me. They were also poor, and some of them, most of them really, had horrible lawyers," she recalls.

This resonated with Michele and sparked something inside her that would eventually lead her to earn her bachelor's degree from Wesleyan University and then a law degree from the University of California at Berkeley. She was ready to make a difference, but where would she begin?

AN INTENTION FOR JUSTICE AND FAIRNESS: A CAREER COMMITTED TO CHANGING COMPANY CULTURE

The childhood experiences that made her want to study the law also led her to choose how she wanted to practice law, at least initially. You could say she set that intention quite early on in her life—to pursue justice and ensure everyone is treated fairly.

She says, "When I decided I wanted to be a lawyer, I decided that I wanted to be a public defender because I did feel strongly that the mere fact that you're poor shouldn't mean that you don't get justice." However, don't think she was naïve; she was a realist. She had no illusions that every person she defended would be wrongfully accused.

> "I believed nobody can do this better than I could."

However, she did believe that everyone should have the same right to have that guilt or innocence determined by the letter of the law.

If someone was guilty or innocent, that person's economic status in no way changed what the US Constitution promised, and she committed to giving every person a strong defense, regardless of what the person's bank account could afford. "I felt very strongly that this young man, typically a young man, standing to my left, despite having given me a nickel, still deserved a $1 million defense. So that's what I tried to provide," she says.

Michele served as a public defender for the District of Columbia for eight years, eventually rising to chief of the trial division there. But she didn't like working in management there and moved on to a small law firm with about 11 or 12 lawyers; there she could continue her criminal defense work, but enjoy the variety of adding civil litigation into the mix.

Michele built a reputation as a strong trial lawyer at boutique and large law firms alike, eventually becoming a top partner in the Washington, DC, office of Skadden, Arps, Slate, Meagher & Flom. She weathered the storm of discrimination and high expectations of being a woman of color in the legal profession, garnering a reputation of undeniable skill and grace and continually climbing the ladder until she heard about a unique career opportunity. It was a job too good to ignore for a woman who fell in love with the New York Knicks as a young girl—the National Basketball Players Association was looking for a new executive director.

Michele grew up with a deep appreciation for the sport. It was common to catch a game of hoops in the neighborhood, and fun to watch. At home, even if she hadn't enjoyed the game, she had little choice. "We had one television. When you have two older brothers, both of whom think they're going to be playing in the NBA—when basketball's on, that's what you watch. So, I love the game," she says.

When Michele heard about the job, she was determined to get it. While some may have been intimidated by the position, she was not. In fact, she remembers, "The more I thought about the fact that I could do it, it encouraged me. I believed nobody can do this better than I could." When she found out she would be interviewed by some of the players, it only added to her excitement.

"When I learned that the players were going to be interviewing the candidates for the position as well, I thought even if I don't get it, I could be interviewed by some of these guys that I loved," she recalls. "But when I started thinking about it, I couldn't stop."

She was driven, she was undaunted, and she truly believed she was the perfect person for the job. She thundered full steam ahead fueled by her personal mantra, in the words of Winston Churchill, "Never, never, never give up."

Michele knew that to make real change for the union, she needed to get buy-in and trust from the players. The union needed to recover from a contentious period that culminated in the firing of its previous executive director after an independent review revealed issues, including questionable hiring practices and financial decisions.

The players needed to understand who she was and how she could help them bring about the change they wanted. During her interviews, she made her intentions known, saying, "If you're serious about it, I'm serious about taking your union back. What you have to do is commit to not allowing whoever gets this job to run your union for you. I will be your trusted advisor, but if you want someone to just go ahead and take this ball and run with it, I'm not interested in that. I'm interested in working as a partnership, and providing you with the best advice that you can get so that you can in fact run your union."

> "That's my job—to earn their trust and let them know they are valued on a professional level."

Michele's intention from earlier in her life, to help people in the courtroom, can be seen in her desire to help the players take their union back. For Michele, having the players running the union was the best way to make a change—to have them advocating for themselves, bringing their personal experiences to the table, building the union they wanted and needed to be happy and healthy during their careers. She made her case in her interviews with players including Stephen Curry, Chris Paul, and Anthony Tolliver. She landed the job.

By putting the players in the driver's seat, Michele not only became an agent of change but also spawned other change agents—

the players themselves—which would eventually create the type of culture the players really wanted.

"The union that I inherited was nothing like the union that exists right now," she says. "I am really proud of where we've taken this one in the last six years."

ADVICE FROM MICHELE

Michele's personal story illuminates a lot of great advice for being an agent of change and living an intentional life. Here are four key pieces of advice to consider as you contemplate making big waves in company culture.

#1: Build Intentional Relationships and Trust and Get Buy-In

People can't get on board with your vision if they don't trust you, so to be an agent of change, you need to get buy-in from others who can help you make your idea a reality. Michele talks about how she had to let the players she worked with, some of the biggest names in basketball, know that she wanted to help bring to life what their view of the union should be: "I literally had to insinuate myself into their lives. Some players were very interested in and excited about my being there, but the overwhelming majority of them weren't. It took a lot of work and time to get where I am now. I remember months going by without having any contact that I didn't initiate. Getting a phone call from a player was a huge deal. Now I get calls from players all the time, and they just kind of say, 'Hey, Michele, what's up?' It took me years to get there. I have to do it all over again with every new group of guys that comes in, because they don't know what the union is. That's my job—to earn their trust and let them know they are valued on a professional level."

As Michele settled into her role, she developed meaningful relationships with the mothers of some of the players, who had nurtured them since they were young players in the schoolyard. She notes: "Most of these players have mothers who are fantastic. Many of them are single moms, and they found a way for their sons' dreams to come true and therefore have the respect of their sons." Building a good relationship with the moms helped Michele to cultivate trust with the players.

#2: Don't Let Others Intimidate You. Insist on Respect

Maybe we should've made this number one, because without it, change isn't possible. Change only comes when you insist on respect. If you aren't respected, you're not in a place to influence. Now that's not to say you need people to approve of you—the respect we're talking about here is the kind that you have to first give yourself: self-respect. You can't waver or let people treat you like you don't matter. You must eschew the impostor syndrome. You deserve to be heard and respected. Michele found that the players she worked with, men who were making millions each year, were at the end of the day very concerned about being respected—and for good reason. Insisting on respect lets people know you are serious, that you won't be taken advantage of or dismissed. To be an agent of change, you must insist on respect.

#3: Motivate Your Team

There are two kinds of motivation, intrinsic and extrinsic. Intrinsic motivation is the type that is motivated by internal reward, that comes from within you. Extrinsic motivation is when you are motivated by things or people outside of you. Michele worked with players who are competitive by nature and are intrinsically motivated to be their best on the court. However, she found that they needed some extrinsic motivation from her when it came to creating the environment they wanted.

She says, "These guys are as competitive as the day is long, but I may need to motivate them to appreciate their power and their leverage when we're in the midst of appropriations or a dispute between the league and a player." Being an agent of change means you have to lead the troops.

> "Live your life professionally in a way where your standards are so high for yourself, you'll be able to walk among people who believe themselves to be giants, when to you they're ants."

Motivation is personal. We are all driven by different things. However, there are a few ways you can tailor basic principles to each person on your team. In the article "9 Super Effective Ways to Motivate Your Team," author Peter Economy, who writes *Inc.* magazine's "The Leadership Guy" column, touches on a few ways you can inspire the members of your team to work for the culture they want.[1] First, create a collaborative environment. This goes back to buy-in and trust; encourage the people on your team to talk it out and bring their ideas to the table. Next, establish clear goals. Be able to put down on paper the sort of company culture you want to bring to life. What do you want to change? How will you change it? Finally, one of the best ways to motivate others is to trust them, and you can do that by avoiding micromanaging. Trust the people on your team with their goals and duties, and they'll turn your extrinsic motivation into their own intrinsic motivation!

#4: You Gotta Do the Work

It's a message you've read repeatedly in these pages, but it bears repeating. You have to do the work. In our conversation, Michele said something very obvious, but very true: "Everybody wants to be Beyoncé, but no one wants to do the work." Think about it; when you're Queen

Bey, you can't settle for "good enough." When you are trying to make real meaningful change, you have to make a major effort. There is no halfway or "I'll get to it later." It's hard work 24/7/365.

Michele also recognizes as not only a woman, but also a woman of color, there's a lot of pressure to "pave the way" and "represent" for those that come after her. It is something that has to be acknowledged, but also something you can't allow to define you. Leaving nothing to chance, Michele's C game is as good as anyone else's A game, but for no other reason than to please herself. She says, "Live your life professionally in a way where your standards are so high for yourself, you'll be able to walk among people who believe themselves to be giants, when to you they're ants." Work hard and have high standards for yourself.

> "Everybody wants to be Beyoncé, but no one wants to do the work."

HOW WILL YOU BECOME AN AGENT OF CHANGE?

Now that you've read about what it means to be an agent of change, how will you become one? Reflect on these questions:

- What change would I like to create in my personal and/or professional life?
- How can I make an intention around this desire?
- How will this change impact me and others?
- What steps do I need to take to begin down this path?
- Whom can I recruit to help with this?

Once you've given these questions some thoughtful consideration, set your intention, and start building an action plan with a timetable for deliverables. Steps should be realistic and quantifiable. Once you have your plan of attack, get others to buy into your vision. *Remember:*

organizational change requires leveraging, analyzing, regrouping, and reflection. You will need to go back to the drawing board repeatedly. You may need to periodically recruit more people. Most of all, revisit your intention and fully commit to your plan. Change agents demonstrate who they are by their intentions and their actions, so stay consistent and strong.

11

TRANSFERABLE SKILLS

Leveraging Your Prized Assets

Devoting yourself to a particular art is invaluable.
The art becomes our vehicle with which we drive down the road of life.
—CHRIS MATAKAS

How do you use what you've got so you can get what you want? Understanding the know-how, gifts, and talents that you have accumulated can go a long way. Most of the time these are transferable skills, and they can help you move through a career—or start a new one!

Transferable skills are any skills you possess that are useful to employers across various jobs and industries. These might include skills such as adaptability, organization, teamwork, strategic agility, critical thinking, or other qualities employers seek in strong candidates. Transferable skills can be used to position your past experience as a lever when applying for a new job, especially if it's in a different industry. However, the types of transferable skills employees are likely to possess are, to a certain extent, defined by their generation. After all, it's not like you'll be faxing memos in our modern, paper-free, tech world.

MILLENNIAL SKILL SETS

Millennials have a different set of professional values and are especially adept at utilizing technology. Their key skills span both the hard and soft variety. Hard skills are those abilities that are easy to quantify, whereas soft skills are considered personality traits or characteristics, often referred to as "people skills."

First, let's talk about the most commonly identified hard skills millennials demonstrate—how tech-savvy they are. Growing up during the tech boom gave millennials a comfort with technology that many people in older generations find enviable. Millennials know digital platforms; they understand not only how you use them but also why you would use one over another. They have a greater knowledge of affiliate marketing, video production, sales, and business analytics. There's also been a huge push in recent years to prioritize math and science, especially for women. More and more women are not just joining but dominating and innovating former notoriously predominately male spaces in programming, coding, blockchain, analytics, and tech entrepreneurship. Hard skills can also be bolstered by formal education, specifically degrees and certifications that underscore millennials' knowledge and mastery of a given subject.

The soft skill strengths that millennials possess include a global mindset, a sense of purpose in their work, and a greater commitment to what they're doing. Other soft skills include creativity, emotional intelligence, adaptability, and comfort working in collaborative environments. *U.S. News & World Report*'s article "8 Skills That Set Millennials Apart at Work" highlights the strengths millennials generally bring to teams.[1] The greatest soft skill they bring may be competent communication.

Here's something to remember that will serve you well as your career develops: Employees who have strong oral communication skills as part of their communication competency will always have an edge over those who prefer to communicate from behind a screen. The power of picking up the phone and having a conversation cannot be underestimated. Some things do not translate well over text or email. Human connection alleviates confusion.

I know it's early, but it's time to grab your journal and do a little self-assessment. Ask yourself the following questions:

- What are your greatest skills?
- What hard skills do you have in your arsenal?

- What soft skills do you excel at?
- Do you have a good balance of hard and soft skills, or are you lacking in one or the other?
- How do your skills help you to realize your intention(s)?

Make a list of your answers now and then come back to them later. Treat this like a dynamic, living list—continue to update it. I'm sure you'll think of more skills by the time we reach the end of the chapter and then still more tomorrow and next week.

Sometimes people feel like they only know one thing, or are stuck in one industry, while others focus on their skill sets and move through jobs and industries by figuring out what they bring to the table. Mimi Valdés is a great example of a woman who took her transferable skills and created a career with impact and intention at its core.

MEET MIMI VALDÉS

If the name Mimi Valdés is familiar to you, it's for good reason. Her career has spanned journalism, music, and film. She's held the editor in chief role at both *Vibe* and *Latina* magazines. Later, she went on to work for super producer Pharrell Williams as his creative director at his multimedia company i am OTHER, conceiving projects such as the long-form video for the blockbuster song "Happy." More recently, she's embarked on a Hollywood career working on critically acclaimed movies.

Perhaps most notably, Mimi played a key role in bringing to the big screen the story of the Black women who helped launch astronaut John Glenn into space in 1962. The 2016 Oscar-nominated film *Hidden Figures* revealed to the world that three Black women, Mary Jackson, Katherine Johnson, and Dorothy Vaughan, were a key part of NASA's mathematical work unit responsible for the successful mission. Long before actual computers did the calculations, "computers" were people who performed critical math needed to enable space-flight. She knew as soon as she began learning about the story that it was a story she had to help tell.

"I was like, wow, we've never seen a movie with this level of female brilliance on the screen before. And then take into account the fact that these are Black women. I knew this was going to be huge for us," she says. "This was going to be such a monumental moment because as we all know, representation matters, right? Most pointedly in the tech industry and STEM careers in general. This is an industry where women have made so many strides, but they haven't been acknowledged."

So how do you go from being a magazine editor, to working with a brilliant singer-songwriter, to bringing a movie to the screen that not only made quadruple the revenue that the movie studio thought it would, but also left a lasting impression on the world about the depths of #Blackgirlmagic? In Mimi's case, she transferred her adept storytelling skills across various projects in different industries.

Mimi's calling to tell stories came early in her life. She was raised in Manhattan's Chelsea projects by her mother and grandmother, her father having died before she was born. Mimi developed an interest in magazines when she was young.

"I was fascinated with magazines," she recalls. "I loved the world that they expose you to. Those windows were a bigger world than what I saw outside my project window or in my neighborhood. I didn't realize that it could be a job though, until much later."

It was a neighbor she babysat for who first made her realize that a magazine career could be a reality. Her mom, whose job at New York University Medical Center entitled Mimi to free tuition at NYU, wasn't having it. So Mimi made a deal of sorts.

She explains: "I was about 11 or 12 years old when I kind of already made the decision that I'm going to try to figure out this magazine thing. My mom heard this and had a meltdown; she hoped I'd be a lawyer. So in order to please her I said, 'Although I'm going to go to college and major in journalism, if I don't get a job in magazines within a year, I'll go to law school.'"

Well, law school never happened. Her experience at NYU cemented the fact that she was on the right track. "I loved the coursework, you know, English and history, anything to do with stories," Mimi recalls. She went on to get a job at *Vibe* as an editorial assistant, launching a 13-year ride that would land her at the top of the magazine's masthead.

Hidden Figures wasn't Mimi's first foray into film. She got involved in the production of the 2015 film *Dope* as coproducer. Even though she was very involved, she wasn't quite sure what that role meant or how her skills transferred to shooting the movie. When filming began, she had planned to hang back, until producer Nina Yang Bongiovi took notice of her unique ability to interact with all the department heads and crew.

"My intention was only to come on set for a week, and by day three, she pulled me to the side and said, 'Clearly your experience being an editor in chief and working with creative people is such an asset. Can you please stay the whole time?'" Mimi recalls. The movie was well received by critics and played at the Sundance and Cannes film festivals.

The experience working on *Dope* and Bongiovi's recognition of her skills, along with her ability to understand what makes a story resonate with people, led Mimi to better understand how her gift and skill at storytelling contributed to the incredible success of *Hidden Figures* and a new intention.

USING INTENTION TO DIVERSIFY THE NARRATIVE

While some intentions can be personal in nature, Mimi's very ambitious intention to bring unheard stories to the masses to enrich culture and understanding was realized, at least for the first time, just a few years ago. A smaller piece of that intention—to shine a light on pioneering Black women through *Hidden Figures*—would set off a butterfly effect. While we all think of it as the hugely successful film that it is, you may not (or may, sadly) believe that only one studio was willing to make it. While the studio executives were very supportive of the project, they felt that if it made $60 million, that would be a huge success. Imagine their surprise when it grossed over $235 million worldwide. Hollywood started to sit up and take notice. People were hungry for new voices and new inspiration. Mimi is determined to bring those stories to the audience.

Mimi's intention had a far-reaching effect and not just in Hollywood, but in the often-undercelebrated Black community. Seeing these three amazing women who accomplished so much in an intimidating area like math, made math instantly more accessible. Mimi reflects on this, saying, "The most important thing to me was that this could be a movie that makes math look cool and hopefully inspires more women, more Black people, more people in general, to pursue these careers and even think of them as sexy."

While the global social impact of *Hidden Figures* is incalculable, Mimi's intention is still deeply her own. She realized and was inspired by what she helped create for herself and for Black women as a whole.

Of course, this is just the beginning of Mimi's long-term intention to bring new narratives to the people. Her intention is enduring while always changing and growing. That's the nature of intention; it evolves with you.

MIMI'S SPECIAL RELATIONSHIP WITH INTENTION: CREATING A RITUAL

As we were talking about intention, Mimi said something that was so compelling that I wanted to share it with you. Mimi has a unique annual approach to intention—her "Start Fresh" ritual. Every year on New Year's Eve, Mimi performs this intention ritual: "I have a tradition," she explains, "where I jump in the shower before the clock strikes midnight. Then, loofah in hand, I figuratively wash away all the bad, all the negativity, and all the things I want to leave behind from this past year. As I rinse it away, I contemplate the new year—what will it bring, what will make me happy, and how will my career grow. The shower gets rid of all the things I don't want to bring into the new year. Then I come out of the shower and put on a completely new outfit that symbolizes what I'll be focusing on in the new year." Clean slate achieved!

Is that brilliant, or is that brilliant? It's simple, sweet, and symbolic, making it easy to do and keep doing.

Could a ritual like Mimi's help you realize your intention? Yes! Rituals have been scientifically proved to work. Think about the rituals you perform now; they seem hardwired, don't they? In an article published in *Scientific American*, "Why Rituals Work," authors Francesca Gino and Michael Norton write about how ritual and intention are natural bedmates. They say, "People engage in rituals with the intention of achieving a wide set of desired outcomes, from reducing their anxiety to boosting their confidence, alleviating their grief to performing well in a competition—or even making it rain."[2] They go on to give examples like Michael Jordan always wearing his University of North Carolina shorts (UNC being his college alma mater) under his Bulls uniform when he played. The most effective types of rituals are simpatias, "formulaic rituals that are used for solving problems such as quitting smoking, curing asthma, and warding off bad luck."[3] However, researchers say that consistently performing any rituals with a particular intention in mind is enough to bring the result to fruition.

So let me ask you, how can you build a ritual around one or more of your intentions? It's not difficult. First, choose your intention, if you have more than one. Be sure you can clearly articulate what you're working toward. Then choose a time frame—do you prefer revisiting your intention daily, weekly, monthly, or annually? Now decide how you will make it a ritual. What will you do when you're setting and revisiting your intention? Consider setting the stage by picking a specific place and time to perform the ritual. Add "props," like candles, or add activities, like meditation, to build your practice. Finally, set your schedule for your intention ritual and stick to it! Adjust when necessary but stay consistent in your practice.

AUTHENTICITY IS A SKILL

We talk a lot about authenticity over these many chapters. We talk about its importance when looking inward as we assess ourselves, we see its value when building relationships with others, and it's a critical element when forming our intentions. However, I want you to think of authenticity in a new way; let's call it "intentional authenticity." You can't take an honest inventory of your skills without being 100 percent authentic. If you aren't good at talking in front of a large group, don't add it to your list as a skill you have. You can, however, be real with yourself, and recognize it's a skill you are currently weak in and then create an intention to improve it.

Mimi recognizes just how important authenticity is in both one's personal and professional life. She says, "I think, first and foremost, you just have to know who you are and what you stand for. You need to know what you're willing to fight for and what you're willing to let go of, because you can't fight all the time. That said, the one thing people should never do is put themselves in a position where they're not their best true self and living their life in accordance with that truth." What do you believe in? What's most important to you? What's something that it would be nice to have, but you aren't going to gamble the farm on it? Knowing yourself is one of the most valuable skills you have.

Authenticity also comes from a place of knowing how you became who you are. Truly knowing that, you can act from a place that honors and respects it. Mimi remembers this and created an intention around it, saying, "I'm always conscious of making sure that I'm providing opportunities for other people, because the reason I'm even here is that people gave me opportunities. I think it's that kind of authenticity I'm so attracted to. I also believe it's so valuable because when you are living authentically, you're able to be your true self not just in your personal life, but in your work life as well."

> "You need to know what you're willing to fight for and what you're willing to let go of, because you can't fight all the time."

Let's take a minute for some introspection and reflection, and do an authenticity check-in. Feel free to answer from the gut this first time, but revisit your answers in the future and see if you can go deeper to unearth even more about your true self. Consider these questions:

- Who am I? What do I stand for? What is most important to me?
- Do I act in line with my authentic self?
- What things do I love about myself?
- What things would I like to work on?
- How do I present my authentic self in my personal life?
- How do I present my authentic self in my professional life?
- How can I bring more authenticity to my everyday interactions?

Need help living authentically and strengthening this transferable skill? Stephen Joseph, PhD, a professor of psychology, health, and social care at the University of Nottingham, in his article "What Are the Three Steps to an Authentic Life?," offers three steps you can employ.[4] The first step is to face up to the truth about yourself, regardless of how disagreeable you may find it. The second step is to resist outside interference from people who would bully or persuade you to believe and act in a way that runs counter to your authentic self. The third and final step is, I think, the hardest: You have to overcome your desire to fit in.

MIMI'S THREE TIPS FOR HONING YOUR TRANSFERABLE SKILLS

In addition to all the other amazing things Mimi has to say, she's laid out a few tips for recognizing your transferable skills, applying them, and enriching them.

#1: Recognize Your Unique Value and Voice

What you bring to the proverbial table is not always school learning and direct, industry-specific skill sets. Mimi tells her own story about not limiting how you define your skills. She says, "I was an editorial assistant, but it was my expertise in hip-hop and its culture that made me feel very empowered. I knew that I was a really valuable asset to the magazine," when talking about her time at *Vibe*. She goes on to say, "I felt like having that one specific skill set, intimate knowledge of hip-hop, made me stand out. I think I was the only one that was going to multiple clubs every night and going to see shows." Her passion for hip-hop became a huge asset. People knew she had her finger on the pulse of it, so they were always asking her questions and coming to her for advice and recommendations. The magazine knew her unique value because of it.

Now that you've read Mimi's example, can you think of one or two of your unique values that you can consider a transferable asset? What passions can you transform into workplace skills? Were you the president of your sorority and known for being able to talk to anyone at any time? Your friendly and comforting demeanor could be ideal for training, client relations, or mediation. Be sure to add these skills to the list you started earlier in the chapter.

#2: Market Your Expertise

There's an old saying, "Don't hide your light under a bushel," and it's applicable here. What's the use of having a unique value if you don't let people know about it? We've touched on this in past chapters when we've talked about personal brand. Make sure your company knows your value. Make sure it's clear to not only your superiors but your coworkers as well.

"Make it clear that you know you're there not just to do the job, but to do the job together," Mimi says. When coworkers and bosses know about your expertise, they can call on you when they need to, giving you more opportunity for collaboration and promoting your ability to work in teams. These same colleagues and supervisors could later sponsor or mentor you, because not only did you have valuable skills, but you were also willing to share them to make everyone better.

Aside from sending an email to the company listing everything you're good at (*please do not do that*), find other ways to display your expertise. Fluent in a language? Let the folks in HR know they can add you to their multilingual employee list. Practice Duolingo at your desk on a break to stay fresh; someone is bound to hear you and ask for details. Get creative to find subtle ways to market your expertise to your boss and coworkers.

#3: Be Intentional About Developing Your Skills

Listen, you aren't going to be good at everything. I know we really want to be the Queen of Everything, but in reality, we just can't be an expert in it all. That's why it's important to be intentional about developing your skills. For instance, Mimi says she wishes she was more financially savvy when she was younger, and reflects on it, saying, "I definitely had a period where I remember being just so confused about money and 401(k)s. I knew I needed to save and invest, but how much should I be saving, and how much should I invest, and in what? It was something I didn't know about, and nobody in my circle at the time knew anything about it. So I definitely would have encouraged myself to just be a little bit more financially savvy when I was younger." Benefit from Mimi's lesson by actively tracking and developing your skills.

Now you can't say, "OK, I am going to improve all my weaker skills. I am going to improve my golf game for company and client retreats. I need to learn Mandarin and improve my Spanish so I have greater opportunities abroad. I am going to become a better speaker, learn how to code, bone up on wine pairings, improve my leadership skills, and take a marketing analytics workshop." Instead, be intentional about your skill development. Go back to your list and identify those skills that are weak and need improvement and that are immediately applicable to your professional or personal success. Are there skills you don't have at all that you feel would grow your value at your current company, or when finding a job a year down the line? Choose the skills that make the most sense, give yourself a timeline, and write out a plan for each. By being intentional with your choices, you'll be able to develop your skills in a meaningful way, making you more marketable and confident.

The hope is, you are feeling empowered knowing you have more professional skills than you previously believed!

· · ·

Now that you've finished digesting Mimi's three tips for honing your transferable skills, let's wrap up this chapter with a quick review:

- How are your lists looking? *Hint:* If you need help, enlist mentors, sponsors, your support circle, and other trusted peers.
- Have you designed an intention ritual? Remember, it doesn't have to be complicated and involved—make it manageable but meaningful for you.
- Are you living authentically? Is it a skill set for you? If not, how can you use your reflections to live more authentically?
- Which of Mimi's tips will you focus on this week or month? Be sure to make a plan with quantifiable steps instead of nebulous statements.

I know that in doing these reflections and exercises, you will uncover talents you never realized were transferable and will find ways to further support your intentions.

12

SMART MONEY

Manage Your Financial Life Like You
Manage Your Social Life . . . Carefully!

Treat your mind like your money;
don't waste it.
—SOPHIA AMORUSO

Is your social life planned out like a boss would? Are you scheduled for a weekend trip to Napa on Friday through Sunday, Tuesday morning breakfast meeting with your mentor, Zoom catch-up with your support circle on Wednesday night, and drinks with your bestie on Thursday night?

If so, it's no surprise! Millennials are "the most diverse, tolerant, connected, educated, and idealistic of all generations," writes Paul Taylor, the former executive director of the Pew Research Center in an article for the Bush Institute journal *The Catalyst*.[1] Millennials' unyielding desire for social connection sets them apart—and it's healthy. Connection feeds you and nurtures you.

However, it's equally important for you to pay as much attention to your financial health as you do to your social life. That's not to say that as a millennial you aren't concerned about money. Of course you are. What's stopping you from financial greatness? Financial education, which is ironic, since education is such a key definer of the millennial generation.

Earlier in this book, we spoke to investor Mellody Hobson, who provided sage advice and inspiration not only around taking control of your career, but around taking control of your personal finances. This element of your life is so important to you and to your ability to manifest your intentions, that I feel strongly about leaving you with more information, advice, and resources that will help you secure a plentiful financial future.

MILLENNIALS AND FINANCES

For a number of years what we've heard about millennials and finances has been grim—and may have come off as judgmental. One of the common narratives is that many millennials are afraid to buy homes because they saw their parents lose them in the 2007–2009 financial crisis. Another common storyline has been that the millennials want to buy a home or invest but can't because they're drowning in student loan debt. There's also the idea that millennials overemphasize spending money on experiences and spending time and money on socializing with friends.

The truth is that there is some validity in all those assertions, but what's not captured in them is the fact that, deep down, many millennials want to build a stronger financial future. Because of some of the challenges that millennials face—like record-high levels of student loan debt and habits that they've adopted—they haven't reached certain milestones at the same rate as older generations, creating a wealth gap. According to an analysis by the St. Louis Federal Reserve, in the fourth quarter of 2020 millennials' average wealth was 11 percent below that of Gen Xers at the same age. But there was encouraging news in the report. As they have aged, millennials are catching up to their predecessors. According to the St. Louis Fed, "While trailing Gen Xers for the beginning of their adult lives, millennials' average family wealth has caught up over the past five years."[2]

Still, the gap is concerning, and it could make it more difficult for some millennials to reach their financial goals. As you may recall, earlier in these pages, some of the women interviewed, including Mimi Valdés and Angela Yee, expressed that they wish they had put more time into learning about money and making plans around it.

To continue catching up and closing this wealth gap, millennials need to spend more time learning about money and investing. A study by the TIAA Institute and researchers at the George Washington University School of Business and Global Financial Literacy Excellence Center asked millennials what they called the "Big Three" financial literacy questions, assessing a basic knowledge of interest rates, inflation, and investment risk. They found that only 16 percent were able to correctly answer all three.[3]

If you're a millennial reading this, don't feel singled out. As you've read throughout this book, many people in older generations had—and still have—the same challenges. To help you take control of your financial future, I spoke to Alexa von Tobel, someone who knows a great deal about money. Together, Alexa and I will give you a quick lesson that will put you on the road to becoming more financially savvy.

MEET ALEXA VON TOBEL

Alexa von Tobel is the founder and managing partner of Inspired Capital, a venture capital firm that she started in 2019. She is also the founder and former CEO of LearnVest, which she began in 2009 as an online guide aimed at increasing women's financial literacy. Later, LearnVest broadened its focus to help both men and women and became a full-fledged financial planning company. In 2015, it was acquired by financial services company Northwestern Mutual. Alexa is also the *New York Times* bestselling author of personal finance books *Financially Fearless* and *Financially Forward*.

Alexa's commitment to providing money management advice and education comes from a deeply personal experience. When she was 14, her father passed away in an accident. Her mother was 48 at the time and was understandably blindsided. In her book *Financially Fearless*, Alexa writes: "Through the haze, I overheard my mom on the phone trying to better understand exactly where we had our financial accounts. On top of dealing with the most heart-wrenching, soul-shaking news she'd ever received, she also had to face another challenge: she would need to start dealing with our finances for the first time in her life."[4] Up until then, her mother had handled the household budget, but her father did all the long-term planning and investments. Upon seeing her mother's stress, Alexa vowed that it would never happen to her. She made an "unbreakable commitment" to learn about money. She took it one step further and set an intention to educate others so they would feel empowered about money as well.

LearnVest was born when Alexa entered and won a startup competition with her idea while still in business school. Her experience observing her mother's stress after her father died developed into a business that would help thousands upon thousands of people learn about, and take control of, their financial future.

THE PSYCHOLOGY OF MONEY

What is the psychology of money? In short, it's the study of our behavior with money. You'll notice as we continue through this chapter that being financially successful comes down to how you behave with money. Taking stock of your behavior is the first step, adjusting it is the second, the third is being consistent, and the final step is observing again and refining where necessary. It's a dynamic process, not a static one.

Your behaviors surrounding money come largely from how you view it. Alexa suggests that you make sure your mindset is attuned to the nature of money and how it's used.

"Think of your financial life as being a critical part of your life. One thing I like to remind people is money is not meant to be worshipped; it's a tool," she explains. "You're not supposed to ignore it, and you're not supposed to obsess over it. It is just a tool that allows you to take care of your family, take care of yourself, protect people, do fun things, and provide yourself with whatever needs you have. One of the things I really like to tell young people is money's not an afterthought. It's part of an everyday use equation."

Knowing that, let's do a quick exercise to identify your money mindset and think about how it influences your behaviors with money. Ask yourself:

- What is money to me?
- Am I a saver or a spender?
- Do I respect money?
- How did my family treat money, and did I pick up behaviors from my family?
- When it comes to money, am I free-spirited or a hard-core budgeter?
- What's more important to me—security or status?

Take some time to journal on these questions over the next few days. Are you financially comfortable and confident with your self-assessment, or are you realizing that something needs to change? No matter which, I think the remainder of this chapter will either help you plot your path or optimize what you're already doing.

START AT THE BEGINNING: FOCUS ON INCOME

Starting a career is a complex and personal process. Among other things, you should consider your long-term prospects. When evaluating your next career move, ask yourself, "Is this a solid career that will generate the income I need to support my future dreams?" We've already talked a lot about what to look for in a career, but let's think about the big question: How do you balance pursuing your passion with the reality of paying the rent? Will your career afford you the material items and experiences you want beyond your regular living expenses?

Alexa received some good advice about just this issue. She says: "I once heard in my thirties, if you can figure out who you are, you can figure out what you love, and then you can do it as soon as possible in your career. You will 100 percent be successful." With that in mind, I invite you to answer these questions:

- Who am I?
- What gets me out of bed in the morning?
- What am I great at?
- What careers are there that intersect my passions and my skills?

Are you already doing what you love? Wonderful! Or do you need help figuring it out? If you need some help identifying careers that may work for you, you can do some research at the website CareerOne Stop (https://www.careeronestop.org). It will give you information on careers, training, and salaries and provide other useful research to help you plan your career trajectory. Other sites like Glassdoor and Fairygodboss, which we learned about in an earlier chapter, also can help.

ALEXA'S TIPS FOR FINANCIAL GREATNESS

Tapping into Alexa's expertise, I asked her for some foundational tips for building financial acumen. She identified four ways millennials can take control of their finances and build for the future.

#1: Make an Intention to Practice Good Financial Hygiene

Just like showering and choosing an outfit every morning, money management needs to be a daily practice. Financial hygiene is the little things you do each day to secure financial success. Alexa says, "It's important for everybody—men, women, young, old. Money management should be a part of your life every day. I honestly think of it as hygiene. If you cannot do the basics of brushing your teeth, taking care

> "You have to be able to manage your financial life. Money is a lifeline."

of yourself, going to the doctor, etc., you can't be an adult. You have to pay your bills, make sure you manage your credit score, and save for retirement. It's hygiene to protect yourself. I don't know why we don't think of it that way as a culture. It's important for everybody of every race, religion, gender, and age. You have to be able to manage your financial life. Money is a lifeline."

A simple budget is the foundation of good financial hygiene. Take an honest look at your monthly income and expenses. Spend some extra time on your spending habits—it's time to be brutally honest. For instance, does your daily morning stop at the coffee shop cost you $5 per day? Do you think, "Well, it's five bucks; I can afford that"? If you go every weekday, that's roughly $100 per month and $1,200 per year. Could you be doing something else with that money? Even cutting down to two coffee stops per week, you could save yourself $720. Are you paying overdraft fees to your bank because you didn't track your debits and charges? Are you paying late fees on credit card or other payments? These are all things that you can avoid, but first you have to get an overview of your spending and then make a plan to control it.

Here's an exercise: Pull all your statements for a month—checking, savings, and credit cards—to track your spending. You'll be surprised by your spending—trust me, everyone is! Pull together all your bills for the month. Put all your spending into categories such as "home," "car," "utilities," and so on. Where can you cut things out? What categories are way higher than they should be? Then find a budget system that works for you. I'd also like to share Alexa's lesson "How to Nail a Great Budget," from her book *Financially Fearless*:

THINK about the big picture. (What are you trying to accomplish?)

INPUT your actual numbers. (What do you have to work with?)

LAYER on the 50/20/30 framework, which divides your paycheck this way: 50 percent for essentials, 20 percent for savings and 30 percent for the rest. (Are you already on track or do you need to adjust?)

REFINE over three months. (Change takes time.)

MONITOR your progress with a daily Money Minute.

Keep in mind that hygiene is a daily practice. If you keep your mind on your money (at least once per day), you'll be building your empire in no time!

#2: Get a Handle on Debt

Paying off debt as soon as possible should be a high priority once you've established a budget. Debt includes everything—car loans, mortgage, student loans, personal loans, and the sneakiest of the bunch, credit cards. Why is credit card debt sneaky?

"Credit card debt is out there, and it's like there's this feeling that since everybody has it, it's OK. It's a massive, massive single point of failure for our financial lives. It hurts your credit score. It creates this feeling of being very behind and makes you feel overwhelmed. The best advice I can give millennials is to avoid credit card debt," Alexa says.

So how do you get out of it? Make a list of your credit card balances and interest charges. On your card with the highest interest, pay as much as you can to bring down the debt, while making minimum payments (or more, if you are able) on your other cards. Remember, don't use the card! Once you've paid off the card with the highest interest, do the same for the card with the next highest interest, and so on. Alexa covers debt extensively in her books, so I'd also recommend reading them if you would like to go deeper into this topic.

#3: Save for Retirement

When you're in your twenties and even early thirties, you probably aren't thinking a ton about retirement, except when you've had a rough day at work and are fantasizing about leaving work behind. I get it! Student loans, rent, and all the other money-sucking expenses that come up while you are establishing yourself are already pinching you. It's hard to add a deduction to your paycheck for retirement, because it's far off and your other expenses are happening right now. However, the earlier you commit to investing for retirement, the better.

> "The second you start saving for retirement, you are compounding interest. It isn't magic; it's math—and it works every time."

Alexa explains: "The second you start saving for retirement, you are compounding interest. It isn't magic; it's math—and it works every time. So the sooner you start, the faster it grows, and it does a lot of the work for you. If you get started early and you can add an extra decade onto your retirement savings, boom, huge exponential growth." Alexa also notes that even if you start small, it will make a big difference in the long run.

Try this exercise. Review what you are currently contributing to your retirement and answer these questions:

- Am I maximizing on my company's matching program (if it has one)?

- Could I cut out my coffee habit (or other discretionary expense here) and increase my contributions right now without feeling the pinch?
- Am I contributing a higher percentage of my bonuses or commissions to my retirement? Can I afford to do so? If this applies to you, see your HR department with questions on how to contribute different amounts for compensation categories.

I bet you'll find a few extra dollars that you can contribute each pay cycle. Trust me, watching that money grow and interest compound gets exciting!

#4: Don't Be Intimidated

Alexa points out one of the biggest barriers for women when it comes to managing and growing your wealth—it can be intimidating!

"Money has a lot of stress and anxiety and shame around it; rip the Band-Aid off, and just say, 'I'm going to give myself a clean slate, and I'm going to get focused on getting really good at this.' The second you start to do that, you're going to feel really good. When you just start learning, people think money is incredibly complicated, and it can be very overwhelming. However, learning the basics is really, really easy," she says. "Pick up a good book, learn the basics, listen to a podcast, but lean in and start to learn about money. You'll start feeling more confident about money, and it will feel really, really good."

· · ·

How are you feeling about money now that we've talked to an expert, and you're armed with information and practical exercises to start down your road to money management and growth? Take the time to really assess your financial situation and see what lessons from this book you can apply to give yourself more financial freedom. I'd highly recommend reading both of Alexa's books; checking out learning tools on Ellevest, an investing platform designed for women and mentioned earlier in Chapter 9; and checking out reputable financial education books, podcasts, and websites.

13

STRONGER TOGETHER

Men as Allies for Female Leaders

We know that when women are empowered,
they immeasurably improve the lives of everyone
around them—their families, their communities,
and their countries.
—PRINCE HARRY, DUKE OF SUSSEX

This chapter is going to be a little different from the 12 that preceded it. So far, we've learned a lot from women about how women have manifested their intentions. It makes sense; who knows a woman's struggles more than another woman?

After centuries of competing for resources, status, and career, there's been a resurgence in women lifting up and supporting other women. It's a happy and overdue change! However, it would be shortsighted to dismiss the other half of the population, the men, who also work toward those same ends. In this fight, they are allies we need to help us facilitate change.

In this chapter, we are going to shift gears to talk about the important role that intentional male allies—whether they are bosses, mentors, or sponsors—can play in your life and career as you build a path toward intentional leadership.

There is a plethora of ways in which men can support women in our day-to-day professional lives, including challenging stereotypes, addressing bias, and providing mentoring, sponsorship, and general support. I am personally grateful for the impressive arsenal of male allies who have served as my confidants, mentors, sponsors, and coaches over the years. I've been fortunate to have had these individuals who have used their personal and professional collateral to aid in my success.

THE ROLE OF ALLIES

Let's step back for a moment. What is an ally? An ally is someone who is not a member of an underrepresented group, but who still takes action to support that group. I think a workplace ally is somebody who wants to be there to support us, and who's willing to accept us for who we are. These allies help bring out the best in us, and sometimes that's just being a sounding board or a listening ear. They aren't afraid to take a stand for the person they support.

Being an ally isn't an easy feat. Some men will suggest a man is selling out for women if he calls sexist behavior into question. Thankfully, allies are brave souls who believe standing tall and speaking out are more important than being in the boy's club.

Forming alliances across gender (and race, ethnicity, religion, and other differences, for that matter) is often framed as a moral imperative, but enlightened leadership understands that it also makes a positive impact on the success of the business. In its research report "Men as Allies: Engaging Men to Advance Women in the Workplace," the Center for Women and Business at Bentley University points out that "it is well established that talented women leaders change the work environment for the better, delivering improved financial results, retention and productivity, and deepening the talent pool."[1]

Research shows that a bigger commitment to gender diversity yields greater results. According to "Diversity Wins: How Inclusion Matters," a 2020 report by McKinsey & Company, "Companies with more than 30 percent women executives were more likely to outperform companies where this percentage ranged from 10 to 30, and in turn these companies were more likely to outperform those with even fewer women executives, or none at all." A substantial differential likelihood of outperformance—48 percent—separates the most from the least gender-diverse companies,[2] Intentional leaders understand that committing to diversity pays dividends; not only is it the right thing to do, but it's critical to a company's growth to fill the room with different faces and perspectives.

In my personal experience, a number of men who have been allies to me have made an immeasurable difference in my career. You may remember some of them from the Introduction of this book, and my previous book, *Climb*. We'll be talking to one of these men, Alex Gorsky, executive chairman of Johnson & Johnson Inc., in this final chapter. I'm excited for you to meet him.

MEET ALEX GORSKY

There is a good chance that you or someone that you know has used or been helped by a product that Johnson & Johnson makes. Alex sits at the helm of a more than 130-year-old company that manufactures a range of brands that you'll find in your home such as skin care lines Neutrogena and Aveeno; over-the-counter medicines and treatments such as Tylenol and Motrin pain relievers; allergy medicines such as Benadryl and Zyrtec; and Visine eye drops. The multinational corporation also makes a range of medicines and devices to address a wide variety of medical conditions and infectious diseases. The company, often referred to as J&J, is one of the world's most valuable companies. It is a component of the Standard & Poor's 100 stock index and in 2020 reported more than $82.5 billion in revenue. Based in New Brunswick, New Jersey, J&J has more than 130,000 employees across the globe in at least 60 countries. I am very fortunate to be able to call Alex my mentor.

I say that not just because Alex runs a highly visible and successful enterprise. Alex doesn't just talk the talk when it comes to diversity and inclusion—he walks the walk. He is the executive sponsor of all J&J employee resource groups, including the Women's Leadership Initiative and the Veteran's Leadership Council. A longtime advocate of inclusion and diversity, Alex has been named one of the "100 Most Inspiring Leaders" by industry publication *PharmaVOICE*. He demonstrates a deliberate and intentional commitment to driving equity in the workplace. In 2018, he won publication *DiversityInc*'s inaugural Global Inclusive Leaders Award. He's known for mentoring and sponsoring people from a wide range of backgrounds and helping them grow their careers. I can attest to this based on my own experience of being mentored and sponsored by Alex over the years. He embodies, in my opinion, all an ally can be. As you learn more about Alex, you'll see how he developed an intention to mentor and develop others with an eye on diversity.

A FOUNDATION OF INTENTIONAL LIVING

Alex is one of six children descended from grandparents who emigrated from Eastern Europe. Intentional living was modeled for Alex and his five brothers and sisters by his parents. His parents created an environment where there was a strong emphasis placed on education and service to others. There was also a demonstrable importance placed on the idea that you can do whatever you'd like to do as long as you're willing to work hard.

"There was an expectation in our family that we should find as many ways as we could to expand ourselves. Whether it was through academics, athletics, or leadership programs didn't matter. All those avenues were ways of learning more about who we were and the world we live in," Alex recalls. His parents were supportive, while also giving him a lot of latitude and free rein to explore. This foundation would later not only support his success but also play a critical part in his intentionality in developing future leaders, especially women.

Alex's mother worked as a teacher's aide to developmentally challenged children, while his father, a Korean War veteran, transitioned from the military to a career in sales for the Gerber Products Co. and rose into the executive ranks there. Alex's father didn't attend the prestigious US Military Academy at West Point, but some of his friends did, and that helped Alex set one of his very first intentions as a youngster. "I think I wrote in my sixth grade journal, which I have somewhere, that I was going to go to West Point when I graduated from high school, and it really became my goal," Alex recalls. He was admitted. His West Point and subsequent experiences serving six years in the US Army began to shape his views on diversity.

"You don't get to choose your roommates, squad members, platoon members—people look different and sound different than you," he explains. "You have to come together as a team to ultimately accomplish a mission. I found that really eye-opening." Whether it was at West Point or during his army service, his experiences made an indelible mark. "Working with people who brought a very different perspective—who are not just of your same crowd—made you understand why diversity is important," he says.

After the army, Alex earned an executive master of business administration degree from the Wharton School at the University of Pennsylvania. In 1988, he landed a job at Janssen Pharmaceutica (now Janssen Pharmaceuticals), which had been acquired by J&J many years before. Over the next 15 years, he advanced through positions of increasing responsibility, culminating in being named chairman and CEO in 2012.

FROM HIS PERSPECTIVE:
CHALLENGES WOMEN FACE IN THE WORKPLACE

Over the years, Alex has mentored many people, including women, whom he has helped rise through Janssen and J&J. He's been a generous ally, continuing to work with people—myself included—after they move onto other organizations. This experience has made him attuned to the challenges women encounter in the workplace.

When it comes to mentoring women, he hones in on helping them navigate two particularly important challenges. These challenges merit a little time to unpack. The first is career pathing, or figuring out the steps you need to take to progress. Another way to think of this would be identifying the goals you need to meet to achieve your intention.

Career pathing is something that many people and organizations struggle with. If a company doesn't proactively assess and communicate career pathing, it may lose talent to a belief that 57 percent of the population has: The only way for people to make their next career move is to leave their current company for another.[3]

Is there one good way to solve this issue? Unfortunately, no. "There's no one answer, so much is situational, depending on the industry, the company, and the circumstance—let alone the individual. You have to understand all those dynamics before you can offer coaching not only about what is the best potential role for you at this point, but also, as you're thinking further down the road, about what other kinds of roles and responsibilities and capabilities you will need to build," Alex says.

Experts suggest that companies make career pathing a priority by adding it to the annual review process. If your company doesn't proactively talk about career pathing, make sure you are revisiting it annually by evaluating where you are in your career and company. Think about where you see yourself in the next 12 months. What skills will you need to develop to get there, and how or where will you get those skills? If you don't have a leader or mentor like Alex to help you figure it out, reach out to your human resources department or your personal support circle for guidance.

The second challenge Alex hears often from the women that he mentors is the universal head-scratcher: How can I impact people?

Alex has found that the women he mentors often wonder, "How do I come across? How can I be more effective in the way that I inspire others to do their best work?" In short, they are asking how they can improve how they lead and influence employees. Alex's advice is pretty straightforward: "I think to be an effective leader, you have to be very comfortable in your skin. It's not as though you put on a uniform and you turn into a leader. You are who you are, and if you're not true to yourself, either people sniff you out as being inauthentic, or you're going to get tired of faking it and being somebody you aren't." He goes on to say that you need to align who you are as a person with who you are as a leader—facets need to be integrated, not compartmentalized. Measure the perceptions you create against your intended perception. If you have an honest appraisal of the impact you have on others, then you can make adjustments that are aligned with your authentic self. This is yet another place where intention helps make you a better leader.

THE ROLE OF INTENTION IN LEADERSHIP

What makes a leader? I'll give you a hint—it's not an impressive title on a business card. Leadership is the ability to guide and influence others toward mutually desired goals. Intentional leadership, on the other hand, takes it a step (or 20) further. The consulting firm The Clearing has a terrific way of defining intentional leadership: "Leaders who operate 'intentionally' act with purpose, forethought, and authenticity in service of achieving sustainable and equitable outcomes. These leaders recognize their attitudes and behaviors set the weather for their teams every day—their presence is their impact."[4] Intentional leadership recognizes the importance of purpose and authenticity, as well as equitable outcomes and the impact the leader's energy and attitude has on the team.

Alex looks at leadership as a dynamic, viewing it as "a skill that has to be practiced." Like any other skill or talent when it's not regularly stretched and challenged, it can fade. He reflects on some of his earliest leadership experiences in the army, which helped him develop his skills: "I was younger and had less experience than some of the soldiers I was tasked with leading. I was able to connect with them, able to engage, and develop empathy, all the while knowing that I was in charge. It's important to remember there's no such thing as leadership without followership." Let that sink in: You need followers to lead. To get followers, you must develop trust and respect. These are seminal lessons for anyone.

How can you become an intentional leader, one who is invested in the team and can lead the team to success? Reflect on times when you were the follower. Which leaders inspired you and supported you? What did they do to earn loyalty? Many of our past experiences can inform us of what to do (and what not to do, too) when we find ourselves at the helm.

So what makes a great leader?

"It's usually someone who inspires us to do more than we could ever imagine or dream of doing ourselves. You know, people who see certain talents or characteristics in us, and then help us bring out the very best of ourselves. They help us manage the more challenging areas but ultimately help us accomplish more than we think we could on our own," Alex says.

Being happy, caring, and decisive, as well as being accountable and responsible to those you lead, are important traits for leaders to develop. But Alex makes it very clear that, most of all, leadership is recognizing talents and ability in others and helping bring them to fruition. It's this attitude and commitment to intentional leadership

> "A skill that has to be practiced."

that makes Alex an irreplaceable ally in a world that still can be resistant to the leadership of women and people of color in general.

"I think that when you bring different perspectives together in that manner, it creates an environment where one plus one plus one can equal seven," Alex says. "After all, if you all look, sound, and talk alike, you probably don't need anybody else there. Sure, it would be a lot easier, because bringing together different perspectives and mindsets sometimes can make us uncomfortable. However, it also opens up the room for creativity and new viewpoints, which opens up a new level of critical thinking that ultimately produces a better outcome."

ADVICE FROM ALEX

Not everyone is as lucky as I am to have found a mentor like Alex. With that in mind, I asked what advice he would give to women about becoming the best leader they can be.

#1: Practice Lifelong Learning

Learning is a critical component to a successful career trajectory and personal development. "I never think, 'I've achieved full success.' There's still plenty of flaws and work in progress that I work on every day," Alex says. "I think it's important to always maintain a certain level of intellectual curiosity. I don't think that the key to success is necessarily always being the smartest person in the room; it's asking the right questions to help the whole room be smarter."

A college education can be a jumping-off point, but think of it as the beginning, not the end, of learning. Alex sums it up perfectly: "I frequently will advise young men and women who are graduating from college, saying, 'Hey, congratulations on your diploma. It's not what you've learned—it's a license to learn more as you go forward.'"

#2: Practice Resilience

Life, as we've all learned, doesn't always go the way we'd like. The difference between those who struggle and those who thrive is a willingness to adjust. Resilience, the ability to recover quickly from difficulties, is a key strength that you should develop for long-term success. Alex explains, "You've got to be prepared for setbacks—all the challenges and unexpected twists and turns that come up along the way."

> "I don't think that the key to success is necessarily always being the smartest person in the room; it's asking the right questions to help the whole room be smarter."

There are lots of ways to build your resilience muscles. The American Psychological Association gives several suggestions such as practicing mindfulness, taking care of your body, strengthening and making new connections, helping others, and looking for opportunities for self-discovery.[5] Embrace a proactive mindset by looking forward, anticipating potential outcomes, and seeing all the angles. When problems seem insurmountable, break them into bitesized, or as I like to think of them, fun-sized, pieces, and knock them out. Keep in mind what we learned in a previous chapter, "Everything is figureoutable."

#3: Practice Authentic Leadership

Alex touched on this earlier, and we've heard it echo throughout the book—be authentic. However, in a leadership context, authenticity faces new challenges. Alex explains: "In large leadership roles, there will always be a certain amount of negativity that you've got to be prepared for. Hence the importance of maintaining your values—the principles that guide you through the storm—and having the resiliency to pick yourself up and learn from your mistakes."

Be prepared to have your morals and values tested. You may think you have to act a certain way to embody a senior title. Maybe in your first job, the CEO was indifferent toward any member of the team that wasn't C-suite. Perhaps the first marketing director you ever met was condescending and talked down to staff. That doesn't have to be you!

Once you achieve the title, make it your own by bringing your unique flavor to the table. Be the kind of leader you would want to follow. Be as intentional in leadership as you are in your personal development. Remember, leadership is a practice. Armed with intention and authenticity, you can be an inspiring and empowering leader.

#4: Practice Self-Care

The concept of practicing self-care is so accepted among millennials today, it almost seems to go without saying. Alex gave this important piece of advice: "Last but not least—take care of yourself. These are challenging jobs. Building the right rituals and habits about the way you care for yourself—that's physically, emotionally, the way you eat, the way you sleep, the way you stay active, the way you achieve balance—is important because you're going to be pulled in so many different directions and you'll face enormous stress. Without that kind of a core strength in ourselves, it's difficult, if not impossible, to succeed. When you bring your best self to work, you're going to bring out the best in everyone."

You've seen Alex's advice around self-care demonstrated in my own story and in the stories of many of the women we spent time with in this book. Taking care of yourself is of the utmost importance. Setting an intention around self-care is the best thing you can do for yourself and your career.

• • •

In closing, keep in mind that no woman is an island. There's a natural feeling that you have to do it all yourself for it to count, but that just isn't true. Don't assume that because people have had different life experiences and circumstances from you, they aren't compassionate or willing to lift you up in any way they can. Engage and embrace allies as you move forward in your personal and professional career. Search out those that actively support and celebrate diversity and invite them to be part of your network. Foster and nurture these relationships. Whenever possible, be an ally yourself and give back all that good mojo you've been getting.

NOTES

Introduction

1. Dimock, Michael, "Defining Generations: Where Millennials End and Generation Z Begins," Pew Research Center Fact Tank, January 17, 2019, https://www.pewresearch.org/fact-tank/2019/01/17/where-millennials-end-and-generation-z-begins/.
2. "Millennials at Work: Reshaping the Workplace," PwC, 2011, https://www.pwc.com/co/es/publicaciones/assets/millennials-at-work.pdf.

Chapter 1

1. Tabaka, Marla, "Setting Goals Isn't Enough: Setting Daily Intentions Will Change Your Life," *Inc.*, July 11, 2016, https://www.inc.com/marla-tabaka/setting-goals-isnt-enough-setting-daily-intentions-will-change-your-life.html.
2. Fry, Richard, "It's Becoming More Common for Young Adults to Live at Home—and for Longer Stretches," Pew Research Center Fact Tank, May 5, 2017, https://www.pewresearch.org/fact-tank/2017/05/05/its-becoming-more-common-for-young-adults-to-live-at-home-and-for-longer-stretches/.
3. Min, Sarah, "More Millennials Are Living at Home Than at Any Other Time This Century," *CBSNews Moneywatch*, May 10, 2019, https://www.cbsnews.com/news/more-millennials-are-living-at-home-than-at-t any-other-time-this-century/.
4. Salata, Sheri, *The Beautiful No: And Other Tales of Trial, Transcendence, and Transformation*, Harper Wave, New York, 2019.

Chapter 2

1. "Women in the Boardroom: A Global Perspective," 6th ed., Deloitte, October 2019.

Chapter 4

1. Park, William, "How Your Friends Change Your Habits—for Better and Worse," BBC.com, May 20, 2019, https://www.bbc.com/future/article/20190520-how-your-friends-change-your-habits---for-better-and-worse.

2. Kiner, Mikaela, "It's Time to Break the Cycle of Female Rivalry," *Harvard Business Review*, April 4, 2020, https://hbr.org/2020/04/its-time-to-break-the-cycle-of-female -rivalry.

3. Robbins, Tony, "How to Surround Yourself with Quality People," tonyrobbins.com, https://www.tonyrobbins.com/stories/business-mastery/surround-yourself-with -quality-people/.

Chapter 5

1. "Perfectionism," *Psychology Today*, https://www.psychologytoday.com/us/basics/ perfectionism.

2. Curran, Thomas, and Hill, Andrew P., "Perfectionism Is Increasing over Time: A Meta- Analysis of Birth Cohort Differences from 1989 to 2016," *American Psychological Association Psychological Bulletin*, Vol. 145, No. 4, pp, 410–429 (2019).

3. Prive, Tanya, "4 Devastating Consequences of a Toxic Workplace Culture," *Inc.*, https://www. inc.com/tanya-prive/4-devastating-consequences-of-a-toxic-workplace -culture.html.

4. Gurchiek, Kathy, "SHRM Research: COVID-19 Takes a Toll on Employees' Mental Well-Being," SHRM.org/*HR Today*, May 11, 2020, https://www.shrm.org/hr-today/ news/hr-news/pages/shrm-research-covid-19-takes-a-toll-on-employees-mental-well -being.aspx.

5. Sandberg, Sheryl, and Thomas, Rachel, "Sheryl Sandberg: The Coronavirus Pandemic Is Creating a 'Double Double Shift' for Women. Employers Must Help," *Fortune*, May 7. 2020, https://fortune.com/2020/05/07/coronavirus-women-sheryl-sandberg-lean -in-employers-covid-19/.

Chapter 6

1. Forleo, Marie, *Everything Is Figureoutable*, Portfolio, New York, 2019.

2. Garcia, Luis, "Why Everyone Needs a Life Coach," *Entrepreneur*, February 12, 2020, https://www.entrepreneur.com/article/345985.

3. Zemple, Jessica, "10 Questions for Picking Your Perfect Life Coach," *Inc.*, January 28, 2016, https://www.inc.com/jessica-zemple/10-questions-for-picking-your -perfect-life-coach.html.

4. "Stress and Gender," American Psychological Association, 2011, https://www.apa.org/ news/press/releases/stress/2011/gender.

5. "5 Things You Should Know About Stress," National Institutes of Health, https://www .nimh.nih.gov/health/publications/stress/index.shtml.

Chapter 7

1. Robison, Jennifer, "What Millennials Want Is Good for Your Business," *Gallup* (blog), March 22, 2019, https://www.gallup.com/workplace/248009/millennials-good -business.aspx.

2. Moniuszko, Sara M., Puente, Marie, and Bravo, Veronica, "Ruth Bader Ginsburg Becomes First Woman to Lie in State: 8 Other Strides She Made for Women," *USA Today*, September 24, 2020, https://www.usatoday.com/in-depth/life/2020/09/24/ ruth-bader-ginsburg-8-things-she-did-womens-rights/3502065001/.

3. Wilkin, Kurt, "The Dark Side of Job Title Inflation," HireBetter, August 22, 2019, https://hirebetter.com/the-dark-side-of-job-title-inflation/.

4. Hess, Abigail Johnson, "Just 0.2% of VC Funding Goes to Black Women Founders. Backstage Capital Founder Arlan Hamilton Wants to Close That Gap," CNBC.com, November 19, 2018, https://www.cnbc.com/2018/11/19/arlan-hamilton-founded-vc -firmbackstage-capital-while-homeless.html.

5. "All In: Female Founders and CEOs in the US VC Ecosystem," PitchBook, 2020, https://files.pitchbook.com/website/files/pdf/2020_All_In_Female_Founders_and _CEOs_in_the_US_VC_Ecosystem.pdf.
6. "Investing in Underrepresented Founders: What We Can Learn from the Data," US Securities and Exchange Commission, August 4, 2020, https://www.sec.gov/spotlight/ sbcfac/sbcfac-learn-from-data.pdf.
7. Clance, Pauline Rose, and Imes, Suzanne, "The Imposter Phenomenon in High Achieving Women: Dynamics and Therapeutic Intervention," *Psychotherapy Theory, Research & Practice*, Vol. 15, No. 3, pp. 241–247 (Fall 1978).
8. "Women in the Workplace," LeanIn.Org and McKinsey & Company, 2020, https:// wiw-report.s3.amazonaws.com/Women_in_the_Workplace_2020.pdf.
9. "Too Few Women of Color on Boards: Statistics and Solutions," Catalyst, 2020, https:// www.catalyst.org/wp-content/uploads/2020/01/WOB_TooFewWomen.pdf.

Chapter 8

1. Fairlie, Robert, and Desai, Sameeksha, "National Report on Early-Stage Entrepreneurship in the United States: 2020," Kauffman Foundation, February 2021, https://indicators.kauffman.org/wp-content/uploads/sites/2/2021/03/2020_Early -Stage-Entrepreneurship-National-Report.pdf.
2. Fairlie, Robert, Desai, Sameeksha, and Hermann, A. J., "National Report on Early-Stage Entrepreneurship in the United States: 2018," Kauffman Foundation, September 2019, https://indicators.kauffman.org/wp-content/uploads/sites/2/2019/09/National Report_Sept_2019.pdf.
3. Castrillon, Caroline, "Why More Women Are Turning to Entrepreneurship," Forbes.com, February 4, 2019, https://www.forbes.com/sites/carolinecastrillon/2019/02/04/why -more-women-are-turning-to-entrepreneurship/?sh=596cc65542a.
4. Torpey, Elka, "New Year, New Career: 5 Tips for Changing Occupations," Bureau of Labor Statistics, January 2017, https://www.bls.gov/careeroutlook/2017/article/new-career.htm.
5. Patel, Mehul, "Hired's 4th Annual 'Global Brand Health Report,'" *Hired.com* (blog), September 22, 2020, https://hired.com/blog/highlights/2020-brand-health-report/.

Chapter 9

1. Kurz, Christopher, Li, Geng, and Vine, Daniel J., "Are Millennials Different?," Finance and Economics Discussion Series, Divisions of Research & Statistics and Monetary Affairs, Federal Reserve Board, Washington, DC, November 2018.
2. Wronski, Laura, "CNBC/SurveyMonkey Poll: International Women's Day 2020," https://www.surveymonkey.com/curiosity/cnbc-international-womens-day-2020/.
3. "Own Your Worth: Women, Wealth and the Path to Financial Independence," UBS, 2020.
4. "Women & Financial Wellness: Beyond the Bottom Line," Merrill Lynch and Age Wave, 2018, https://www.ml.com/women-financial-wellness-age-wave.html.
5. Horowitz, Juliana Menasce, Igielnik, Ruth, and Kochhar, Rakesh, "Trends in Income and Wealth Inequality," Pew Research Center, 2020, https://www.pewresearch.org/ social-trends/2020/01/09/trends-in-income-and-wealth-inequality/.
6. Oxfam, "Time to Care: Unpaid and Underpaid Care Work and the Global Inequality Crisis," January 2020.
7. Bhutta, Neil, Chang, Andrew C., Dettling, Lisa J., and Hsu, Joanne W., "Disparities in Wealth by Race and Ethnicity in the 2019 Survey of Consumer Finances," FED Notes, Federal Reserve, September 28, 2020, https://www.federalreserve.gov/econres/ notes/feds-notes/disparities-in-wealth-by-race-and-ethnicity-in-the-2019-survey-of -consumer-finances-20200928.htm.

8. Noble, Barbara Presley, "A Few Thousand Women, Networking," *New York Times*, March 27, 1994.

Chapter 10

1. Economy, Peter, "9 Super Effective Ways to Motivate Your Team," *Inc.*, March 18, 2016, https://www.inc.com/peter-economy/9-super-effective-ways-to-motivate-your-team .html.

Chapter 11

1. Koenig, Rebecca, "8 Skills That Set Millennials Apart at Work," *U.S. News & World Report*, October 29, 2018.
2. Gino, Francesca, and Norton, Michael I., "Why Rituals Work," *Scientific American*, May 14, 2013.
3. Ibid.
4. Joseph, Stephen, "What Are the Three Steps to an Authentic Life?," *Psychology Today* (blog), November 3, 2017, https://www.psychologytoday.com/us/blog/what-doesnt -kill-us/201711/what-are-the-three-steps-authentic-life.

Chapter 12

1. Taylor, Paul, "It's a Millennial World Now: Twelve Things to Know," *The Catalyst*, No. 3, Summer 2016, https://www.bushcenter.org/catalyst/next-generation/taylor-its-a -millennial-world.html.
2. "Generational and Age Household Wealth Trends and Wealth Inequality," Federal Reserve Bank of St. Louis," https://www.stlouisfed.org/household-financial-stability/ the-real-state-of-family-wealth/generational-and-age-household-wealth-trends-and -wealth-inequality.
3. Bolognesi, Andrea, Hasler, Andrea, and Lusardi, Annamaria, "Millennials and Money: Financial Preparedness and Money Management Practices Before COVID-19," *Research Dialogue*, No. 167, August 2020, TIAA Institute, https://www.tiaainstitute .org/sites/default/files/presentations/2020-08/TIAA%20Institute_Millennials%20 and%20Money_RD167_Lusardi_August2020_0.pdf.
4. von Tobel, Alexa, *Financially Fearless: The LearnVest Program for Taking Control of Your Money*, Penguin Random House, New York, 2013.

Chapter 13

1. Foster, Trish, "Men as Allies: Engaging Men to Advance Women in the Workplace," Research Report, Center for Women and Business at Bentley University, Spring 2017, https://bentleydownloads.s3.amazonaws.com/cwb/Bentley_CWB_Men_as_Allies_ Research_Report_Spring_2017.pdf.
2. Dixon-Fyle, Sundiatu, Dolan, Kevin, Hunt, Vivian, and Prince, Sara, "Diversity Wins: How Inclusion Matters," McKinsey & Company, May 19, 2020, https://www .mckinsey.com/featured-insights/diversity-and-inclusion/diversity-wins-how -inclusion-matters#:~:text=Our%202019%20analysis%20finds%20that,in%20 2014%20(Exhibit%201).
3. Ginac, Linda, "Why Career Pathing Is Vital to Your Talent Management Strategy in 2019," LinkedIn, January 7, 2019, www.linkedin.com/pulse/why-career-pathing-vital -your-talent-management-2019-linda-ginac-ceo/.
4. Peterson, Morgan, "How to Embody Intentional Leadership," The Clearing (blog), https://dev2021.theclearing.com/insights/how-to-embody-intentional-leadership/.
5. "Building Your Resilience," American Psychological Association, 2012, https://www .apa.org/topics/resilience.

INDEX

ABOUT THE AUTHORS

Michelle Gadsden-Williams is the Managing Director and Global Head of Diversity, Equity and Inclusion for BlackRock. She is an award-winning global diversity executive, author, and philanthropist with more than 25 years of experience as an advocate for equality within corporate America and a thought leader around diversity and inclusion. Michelle is a seasoned diversity practitioner with experience working in the consumer goods, pharmaceutical, and financial services industries before transitioning to professional services in 2017.

Photo by: Manuela Rana

Michelle is the former Managing Director of Inclusion & Diversity for Accenture North America. She provided strategic direction and thought leadership and championed the development of an inclusive environment by integrating diversity practice into all aspects of the business. She has held positions of global responsibility in the diversity management arena, living in Switzerland for close to 10 years of her corporate career, and managed staffing functions for large multinational corporations such as Credit Suisse, Novartis, and Merck & Co, Inc. Prior to her tenure at Merck & Co., Inc., Michelle also held positions in human resources and product development at Phillips-Van Heusen Corporation (now PVH), headquartered in New York City and Wakefern Food Corporation, headquartered in New Jersey.

Michelle has acquired a multitude of community service awards and accolades for her work as a diversity practitioner. She has been recognized by *Black Enterprise* as one of the Top Executives in Corporate Diversity for 2019, 2018, and 2017. The Reverend Al Sharpton recognized Michelle as a 2016 honoree at the National Action Network "Women of Power" Luncheon, an honoree at the Black Institute Awards Gala in NYC, and a 2015 *Ebony* magazine Power 100 honoree. Throughout her career, Michelle has been profiled in *Black Enterprise* magazine, *DiversityInc*, *Diversity Executive*, *Ebony*, *Essence*, *Fortune*, *History Makers*, *Heart & Soul*, *Jet*, *New Vision*, *Science* magazine, *Sister to Sister*, the *New York Times*, the *Wall Street Journal*, and *Target Market News*, and she was recognized as one of 40 Outstanding Executives Under 40 in America in 2006 by the *Network Journal*. Her other notable tributes include being named the 2010 recipient of the Maya Way Award for Diversity Leadership by the incomparable Dr. Maya Angelou, receiving the 2008 Harvard Black Men's Forum Businesswoman of the Year Award, accepting the Rainbow Push Coalition's Bridge Builder Award by the honorable Reverend Jesse L. Jackson, and being recognized with an honorary Doctorate of Humane Letters degree from Kean University for her outstanding personal and professional accomplishments in the field of diversity and inclusion. In 2013 Michelle was appointed as a member of the Global Advisory Council on Gender Parity for the World Economic Forum in Davos, Switzerland.

Michelle earned a BS in Marketing, a BA in Communications from Kean College of New Jersey, and an MS in Organizational

Dynamics from the University of Pennsylvania. She is a proud member of Alpha Kappa Alpha Sorority Incorporated and the Executive Leadership Council. Michelle serves on several boards including the Jackie Robinson Foundation, and is a member of the Women's Leadership Board of the John F. Kennedy School of Government at Harvard University. Michelle lives in New York City.

Erika Roman Saint-Pierre is editor in chief of Culturatti Ink, an indie publishing house that works to create a platform for new, unheard authors. She has ghostwritten dozens of bestselling books on a wide variety of topics including business, finance, corporate culture, leadership, and insurance. Her ghostwritten work has appeared in such magazines as *Forbes*, *Black Enterprise*, and *Money*. She is the recipient of three *Detroit Free Press* awards.